DISCIPLINES OF THE SPIRIT

Other Titles by Howard Thurman

The Centering Moment
The Creative Encounter
Deep is the Hunger
Deep River and the Negro Spiritual Speaks of Life and Death
Meditations of the Heart
Temptations of Jesus
The Growing Edge
The Inward Journey
The Luminous Darkness
Jesus and the Disinherited
The Mood of Christmas
The Search for Common Ground
For the Inward Journey
A Strange Freedom

Related Title
Howard Thurman: Mystic as Prophet

DISCIPLINES
OF THE SPIRIT

Howard Thurman

Friends United Press
Richmond, Indiana

Friends United Press
IO 1 Quaker Hill Drive
Richmond, IN 47374

Harper and Row First Edition 1963
Friends United Press First Edition 1977
Tenth Printing 2003

Library of Congress Cataloging-in-Publication Data

Thurman, Howard, 1900-1981.
    Disciplines of the spirit / Howard Thurman.
        p. cm.
    ISBN 0-913408-35-2
        1. Devotional literature. I. Title.

BV4832.2.T527 2001
248.4—dc21   2001033631

To the students in my course on
Spiritual Disciplines and Resources,
1953-1962

CONTENTS

7

FOREWORD

THE PURPOSE OF THIS BOOK IS TO EXAMINE CERTAIN SPECIFIC aspects of human experience. These aspects are chosen because of their universality and because of their significance for tutoring the human spirit. There are five such areas included in the discussion: commitment, growth, suffering, prayer, and reconciliation.

Most of the material here discussed, except the chapter on reconciliation, has been dealt with in a limited way in the Smith-Willson Lectures given at Southwestern College in November 1960, and the Willson Lectures at Nebraska Wesleyan University in 1961. I wish to express my appreciation to the faculties and student bodies of these two institutions for their generous response to the ideas discussed in the lecture series.

During the past nine years, as a part of my teaching responsibility as Professor of Spiritual Disciplines and Resources in the Graduate School of Theology, Boston University, I have experimented with a wide variety of methods for teaching in this field. I wanted to utilize the raw materials of daily experience as the time and the place of the encounter with God. To the extent to which this could be done, any experience would place the individual in candidacy for spiritual awareness and insight. Finally the course divided itself as follows. The first semester, a study of religious experience, and particularly Christian religious experience. The second semester, a study of suffering, tragedy, and love as the disciplines of the spirit through which an individual may be ushered into the Presence of God. Much of the material in the pages of this book has been winnowed out of the collective quest in which

9

several generations of students and I have engaged. During this same period, in my position as Dean of Marsh Chapel, many of these ideas were explored from the pulpit.

A very particular word of appreciation and recognition must be set down here for four books which have been of special significance to me in my discussion:

1. *The Problem of Pain*, by C. S. Lewis, particularly the quotation I have used from his chapter on "Heaven."

2. *God in Us*, by Miles Lowell Yates. I have found few books more stimulating in my own spiritual search than this series of informal lectures given by Dr. Yates to his students at General Seminary in a course entitled "Ascetical Theology." There is a residue of spiritual wisdom in this book upon which I have drawn for my own soul's nourishment.

3. What Dr. Yates' *God in Us* has meant to my spirit, the third book, *The Meaning of Human Existence* by Leslie Paul, has meant to my mind. I do not deny but gladly express my gratitude for the influence of these two books, particularly, on my own thinking.

4. The fourth book is a novel by Carl Ewald, *My Little Boy, My Big Girl*. I dare not comment on it except to suggest to any person who wishes to enlarge his capacity for feeling life to read it.

A personal word of appreciation also goes to Sydna Altschuler, who, during the two-year period of my leave from Marsh Chapel for a wider ministry in the United States and abroad, is working with me as Research Secretary. She has done both the laborious part of typing the manuscript and made many valuable suggestions in the course of its final preparation.

Finally, my thanks to my daughter, Anne Thurman Chiarenza, copy editor in the International Program in Taxation of the Harvard Law School, for reading the entire manuscript and making many significant and useful comments.

HOWARD THURMAN

Marsh Chapel, Boston, Massachusetts
July, 1963

DISCIPLINES OF THE SPIRIT

I

COMMITMENT

THE MEANING OF COMMITMENT AS A DISCIPLINE OF THE BODY IS
not far to seek. The theme is ancient, as old as self-consciousness
in the life of man. It is a part of the wisdom of the body, one of the
abiding characteristics of life, so biologists tell us, in all its manifestations. At the core of life is a hard purposefulness, a *determination*
to live. There is something dogged and irresistible about the
methodical way life pounces upon whatever may be capable of
sustaining it, and will not release it until its own sustenance is
guaranteed or fulfilled.

A simple but dramatic illustration can be seen by any observer
in the world of nature. The roots of trees spread out in many directions—seeking, always seeking the ground of existence for themselves. Many years ago when I lived in Oberlin, Ohio, I noticed
workmen digging a large hole in the street in front of my house.
When I went out to watch what was going on, I saw that a large
section of sewer pipe had been exposed; around it and encircling it
was a thick network of roots that had found their way inside the
pipe by penetrating the joints in many places. The tree was more
than four hundred yards to the other side of the house, but this did
not matter to the roots. They were on the hunt—for life.

This phenomenon is all the more interesting because it seems, so

13

to speak, involuntary and automatic—that is, self-propelled. The
initiative is not planned, or borrowed from the outside, but rather
seems to be a part of life itself. Indeed, the most fundamental
characteristic of life is its search for nourishment. If this be true,
then the individual in his experience with commitment is not intro-
ducing into the picture an element that is foreign or unknown to
the basis of life. Rather, in the basic conditions of its life the
organism knows in a very profound and far-reaching way the discipline of commitment. Its whole existence depends upon the singleness of this kind of demand—the demand for food, for survival.

Let us examine this further. Life is *alive;* this is its abiding
quality as long as it prevails at all. The word "life" is synonymous
with vitality. Of course we are aware that individual forms of life
around us are living things. In your own household you know that
your cat, or dog, or canary, or rosebush, are alive. You know that
your child, or husband, or wife, or friend, are alive as you relate to
them within a living context. This is obvious. We are so conscious
of the fact of each individual expression of life about us that the
simplest and most wonderful fact of all is passed by. And what is
that? The fact that life itself is alive, has the persistent trait of
living—that any and all living things continue to survive as long
as that essential vitality is available to them.

All this may be said without any ability on our part to define
precisely what life is. In an article in the *Scientific American*
George Wald, discussing "Innovation in Biology," has said,

> Biologists long ago became convinced that it is not useful to define
> life. The trouble with any such definition is that one can always con-
> struct a model that satisfies the definition, yet clearly is not alive. And
> of course we do not ever measure life. We can measure many of its
> manifestations accurately; and we combine those with others that we
> observe, but perhaps cannot measure, to make up our concept of what
> it means to be alive. The life itself is neither observed nor measured. It
> is a summary of and judgment upon our measurements and observa-
> tions. What biologists do about life is to recognize it.[1]

[1] *Scientific American*, September 1958, p. 113.

Thus far we have dwelt on only one main point, and that is that the built-in characteristic of all forms of life is to seek always to keep free and easy access to the source of vitality or aliveness in which all life finds its abiding security. The process by which a particular form of life does this constitutes the nature and type of that organism's discipline. To say that this is a living universe is to say that life itself is alive and that this aliveness expresses itself always in seeking—yes, in goal-seeking. Here the expression is not metaphysically or even morally teleological but connotes, rather, the fact that in the effort of any particular form of life to sustain itself, it does so with reference to ends, at its own level. To state this in another way one may say that life seeks to fulfill itself, that is, to "live itself out." The point is, then, that life wherever it is found is trying to live itself out, or actualize its unique potential.

The bearing of this concept on the discipline of growth will be developed in another chapter. For our purpose here, it is sufficient to point out that the lines along which a particular form of life maintains access to its source of nourishment and vitality involve certain patterns of behavior which, when established, become descriptive of that organism's "method." In other words, the method or structure itself defines the conditions the organism must meet if it is to survive, to live. When the conditions are met, sustenance for the process of life becomes available. Because a fish has gills, it cannot get its oxygen neat but must extract it from water. A man takes his oxygen neat because he has lungs instead of gills.

Precisely what does this mean? Where the conditions for the release of vitality are met, the vitality becomes available, and this is automatic. That is, to the observer it seems automatic. If we were to understand fully what is at work we might find it to be some special kind of consciousness. Who knows? Jesus referred to the earth as being automatic—it brings forth of itself. In any case, when a seed is planted in the soil, if the seed is healthy and the conditions of soil and climate generally satisfactory, then it sprouts. Life becomes manifest. There seems to be available to the seed, at a point in time, all the energy and vitality it can accommodate in its unfolding. It should follow, then, that if the conditions are not met the energy is not available. Any farmer understands how this works. Any housewife who raises plants in the window is acquainted with what is happening here. When a person is said to have a "green thumb" we mean that he or she seems to have an instinctive ability to set up good conditions for growth—it may be a certain feeling for the right depth at which to plant, or a sense of rightness as to soil, moisture, or the happy combination.

But the real magic is the magic of growth itself. There is a discipline at work here. Energy is available for the seed or organism—but under certain given conditions. It does not matter how simple or complex they are, or how self-conscious or lacking in any kind of consciousness; the process itself has to be followed. In the following, in the obedience to the process, the discipline is apparent. It does not matter what variation there may be in the way the means of life are channeled into the organism or living cell, but they must be channeled if life is to continue, and within very definite lines, according to observable conditions. Always there is the possibility of finding new channels and hitherto unexplored conditions of life—this is the essentially creative possibility wherever life appears. But the basic fact remains. If life is to manifest itself in a particular form, it poses the conditions, the discipline, essential to that end. A particular form of life is committed to a *way* of survival, a *way* of keeping alive. When this no longer operates, when the line of communication is broken and the organism is cut adrift, death is automatic.

The German mystic, Meister Eckhart, implied in his teachings that the conditions upon which God enters a man's life are as automatic as the principle outlined above. He insists that, to the extent that a man rids himself of creatureliness, to that extent God *must* enter his life. When creatureliness gives way, God comes in automatically. We appear to be face to face with a principle of mechanics. Fortunately, Eckhart has much more to say about the relationship between the Godhead and the soul of man than can be shown or even suggested here. But there is much to be said for the recognition of what may be regarded as a *general law* of spiritual life.

The meaning of commitment as a discipline of the spirit must take into account that mind and spirit cannot be separated from the body in any absolute sense. It has been wisely said that the time and the place of man's life on earth is the time and the place of his body, but the meaning of his life is as significant and eternal as he wills to make it. While he is on earth, his mind and spirit are domiciled in his body, bound up in a creature who is at once a child of nature and of God. Commitment means that it is possible for a man to yield the nerve center of his consent to a purpose or cause, a movement or an ideal, which may be more important to him than whether he lives or dies. The commitment is a self-conscious act of will by which he affirms his identification with what he is committed to. The character of his commitment is determined by that to which the center or core of his consent is given.

This does not mean, necessarily, that the quality and depth of a man's commitment are of the same order as what he is committed to. There is a dynamic inherent in commitment itself which seems to be independent of what the commitment is focused on. This is an important distinction, always to be borne in mind. Here again we encounter the same basic notion discovered above: there seems to be a certain automatic element in commitment, once it is set in motion. There are a mode of procedure and a sense of priority— one might say, an etiquette and a morality—that belong automatically to this kind of experience, once it becomes operative. In other words, once the conditions are met, energy becomes available in accordance with what seems a well-established pattern of behavior. What is true for plants and animals other than man seems to be true for man. There are many complexities introduced as we observe the pattern at the level of mind, but they must not confuse the basic, elemental fact. When the conditions are met, the energy of life is made available.

In the larger sense, something amoral seems to be at work here.

It is as if the law of life were deeper than the particular expression of self-consciousness in man. It is clear, for instance, that there is no difference between the basic conditions that cause strawberries to grow and the basic conditions that cause poison ivy to grow. Whatever the prerequisites for each, once they are met, the energy of life begins to flow with creative results. The fact that strawberries are a delight to the taste, and nutritious, while poison ivy is irritating and disturbing to man, is beside the point. It is rightly observed that life does not take consequences into account. Each plant meets the conditions for life, and each is supported and sustained.

Serious problems arise when the same principle operates in the conscious activities of man. There is a sense, alas, in which it is true that the wicked do prosper. When a man who has an evil heart gives the nerve center of his consent to evil enterprise, he does receive energy and strength. The most casual observation confirms this in human experience. There is a vitality in the demonic enterprise when it becomes the fundamental commitment of a life. However, the Christian view insists that ultimately the evil enterprise will not be sustained by life, for the simple reason that it is *against* life. What is against life will be destroyed by life, for what is against life is against God. Nevertheless, there is a time interval when nothing is in evidence that can distinguish the quality or integrity of an evil commitment from a good one. This is at least one of the important insights in the Master's parable of the wheat and the tares. There is a period in their growth when they cannot be distinguished or separated from each other. Ultimately the wheat bears fruit proper to itself, and the tares are only tares. But meanwhile the issue is not clear, not clear at all. Again, the Master says that God "makes his sun rise on the evil and the good, and sends rain on the just and the unjust." We seem to be in the presence of a broad and all-comprehending rhythm. There is a logic and an order in the universe in which all living things, at least, are deeply involved.

It remains now to examine the bearing of this fundamental trait of the life process on the meaning of commitment—the act by which the individual gives himself in utter support of a single or particular end. Energy and vitality are apparently not spread around on the basis of a general gratuity; over and above what is given for the mere manifestation of life, there are conditions inherent in the process. When these are met, something happens, energy starts moving, pulsing, becoming manifest in accordance with the form of life that has fulfilled the conditions. In the experience of mankind, the attitude or act that triggers this release of fresh vigor and vitality is singleness of mind. This means surrendering the life at the very core of one's self-consciousness to a single end, goal, or purpose. When a man is able to bring to bear upon a single purpose all the powers of his being, his whole life is energized and vitalized. This is the same principle we have already seen in operation. It shows itself wherever life is manifest. We may expect to find it at work in man's religious experience. In fact, it is my view that the general insight becomes profoundly particularized in religious commitment and that the "general law" reaches its apotheosis in man's religious experience, in the surrender of his life to God. This is the focal point to which all the other manifestations of the insight quietly call attention.

In Christianity there is ever the central, inescapable demand of surrender. The assumption is that this is well within the power of the individual. If the power is lacking, every effort must be put forth to find out what the hindrance is. No exception is permissible. "If the eye is a hindrance, pluck it out . . . if the arm is a hindrance, cut it off." Whatever stands in the way of the complete and full surrender, we must search it out and remove it. If a bad relationship is a hindrance, one must clean it up. In other words, whatever roadblocks appear, the individual must remove them. The yielding of the very nerve center of one's consent is a private, personal act in which a human being, as sovereign, says "Yes." The ability to do this, to say "Yes," is not the result of any special talent, gift, or endowment. It is not the product of any particular status due to birth, social definition, race, or national origin. It is not a power one can exercise only if given the right by one's fellows. It is not contingent upon wealth or poverty, sickness or health, creed or absence of creed. No, the demand is direct and simple: Surrender your inner consent to God—this is your sovereign right—this is your birthright privilege. And a man can do it directly and in his own name. For this he needs no special sponsorship. He yields *his* heart to God and in so doing experiences for the first time a sense of coming home and of being at home.

Here we look squarely into the face of the demand of the Master concerning the Kingdom of God and the meaning of discipleship. It is expressed thus:

And a scribe came up and said to him, "Teacher, I will follow you anywhere"; Jesus said to him, "Foxes have holes, wild birds have nests, but the Son of man has nowhere to lay his head.". . . Another of the disciples said to him, "Lord, let me go and bury my father first of all"; Jesus said to him, "Follow me, and leave the dead to bury their own dead." MATT. 9:19-22

For where your treasure lies, your heart will lie there too. The eye is the lamp of the body: so, if your Eye is generous, the whole of your body will be illumined, but if your Eye is selfish, the whole of your body will be darkened. And if your very light turns dark, then—what a darkness it is! No one can serve two masters: either he will hate one and love the other, or else he will stand by the one and despise the other—you cannot serve both God and Mammon. . . . Seek God's Realm and his goodness, and all that will be yours over and above. MATT. 6: 21-24, 33

Oswald McCall gives an exciting dimension to the concept in these words:

Be under no illusion, you shall gather to yourself the images you love. As you go, the shapes, the lights, the shadows of the things you have preferred will come to you, yes, inveterately, inevitably as bees to their hives. And there in your mind and spirit they will leave with you their distilled essence, sweet as honey or bitter as gall . . .

Cleverness may select skillful words to cast a veil about you, and circumspection may never sleep, yet you will not be hid. No.

As year adds to year, that face of yours, which once lay smooth in your baby crib, like an unwritten page, will take to itself lines, and still more lines, as the parchment of an old historian who jealously sets down all the story. And there, more deep than acids etch the steel, will grow the inscribed narrative of your mental habits, the emotions of your heart, your sense of conscience, your response to duty, what you think of your God and of your fellowmen and of yourself. It will all be there. For men become like that which they love, and the name thereof is written on their brows.[2]

2.

Now we are ready to deal with the working paper of commitment: this is a living world; life is alive, and as expressions of life we, too, are alive and sustained by the characteristic vitality of life itself. God is the source of the vitality, the life, of all living things. His energy is available to plants, to animals, and to our own bodies if the conditions are met. Life is a responsible activity. What is true for our bodies is also true for mind and spirit. At these levels God is immediately available to us if the door is opened to Him. The door is opened by yielding to Him that nerve center where we feel consent or the withholding of it most centrally. Thus, if a man makes his deliberate self-conscious intention the offering to God of his central consent and obedience, then he becomes energized by the living Spirit of the living God.

Let me hasten to point out that this principle does not exhaust all the possibilities. There seem to be occasions, or better, persons, who have the gift of the Spirit where there is no awareness of any act of commitment initiating it. They are the "once born" souls. Their openness to God is one with their own self-consciousness—to share His life and be flooded by His presence is natural to them.

There is another consideration that must be borne steadily in mind. The working principle we are thinking of has nothing to do

[2] Oswald W. S. McCall, *The Hand of God* (New York: Harper & Brothers, 1957), pp. 122-23.

with the question of merit or demerit. When the conditions are met, the individual does not "merit" the energizing strength of the life of God. No, the point is that man's relation to life occurs within a responsible framework—he lives and functions in an orderly context, an essential milieu in which order and not disorder is characteristic. The vast creative mood of existence *is* creative, not chaotic. There is an essential harmony in all existence, and the life of every living thing shares in it. Man co-operates with the Spirit of God by making himself open and available to it. And this fact is crucial. A man may elect not to do this and thereby create for himself many problems of inner chaos and confusion; these may or may not be assessed as such.

The autonomy of the individual must not be denied. It would seem to follow, then, that if the individual meets the conditions, the results ensue automatically. Let us take another look at Meister Eckhart's idea. If we reduce commitment to a mechanical process, there is a denial of other prerogatives and aspects of personality. Commitment viewed in such exclusive terms becomes a manipulative device rather than the door through which man enters into a *good* relationship with God. The yielding of the deep inner nerve center of consent is not a solitary action, unrelated to the total structure or context of the life. It is not a unilateral act in the midst of other unilateral acts on the part of the individual. It is, rather, an ingathering of all the phases of one's being, a creative summary of the individual's life—it is a saturation of the self with the mood and the integrity of assent. Something total within the man says "Yes." It is a unanimous vote and not a mere plurality. It is the yielding of mind, yet more than mind; it is the agreement of the self, expressed in an act of will—yet more than will; it is the sensation of all the feeling tones—yet more than emotions. Despite this ramification, the act of commitment may pinpoint a certain moment in time, or a certain encounter in given circumstances, or a place, or an act of decision that stands out boldly on the horizon of all one's days—the roots spread out in all dimensions of living.

It is for this reason that what one sees as true in a moment of great insight or lucid encounter must be *experienced* as true. This takes time—the conquest spreads over a lifetime.

And all along the way one is hounded by the possibility of having the total affirmation canceled out, sometimes by the overwhelming power of a single act of fundamental contradiction. But the initial moment of surrender is crucial, for it does provide a rallying point as well as a source of referral. When I was a boy we used to sing a song: "If Satan says I don't have grace, I'll take him back to the starting place." For all the journeys of all their days, the time and place of encounter and surrender have been beacons for pilgrims. Moses invaded by the Presence of the great "I AM" before the burning bush—Abraham with Isaac on the lonely height— Jesus coming up out of the water of the Jordan when the Spirit descended like a dove—Paul crying out in the exquisite agony of surrender on the Damascus Road. No—this is not the total story, but it is the moment when all the votes begin to say one thing. And this is the essence of commitment.

The importance given to the conversion experience in Protestant Christianity cannot be separated ultimately from the importance and significance of commitment. Conversion, in Christianity, signifies that there was a moment in the life of the individual when he felt himself convicted of sin. In such a crisis he was able by the grace of God to renounce his past life and accept a new way as one moving dramatic action of his spirit. For many this is the encounter with the living Christ, and in His name or in His Spirit they go forth into newness of life. In recent years there has been a radical decline in such emphasis. There are those who feel that the decline in spiritual vitality in the modern church is due to a lack of this kind of religious experience.

The conversion experience, however it may be interpreted, is the moment when at the depths of his being a man says "Yes" to the will and the rule of God in his life—the moment when he is cleansed, his life redeemed from his old ways, and his feet set on a new path. At such a time the world seems different because of the shining light that glows within him. George Fox says that after such an experience, to him "all the world had a new smell." In the church of my childhood we sang an ancient song:

> *My feet looked new,*
> *My hands looked new,*
> *The world looked new,*
> *When I came out the wilderness,*
> *Leaning on the Lord.*

Such an experience, marking the moment of commitment, provides not only a point of referral for subsequent life but also a basis for integrated behavior. Something seems to be established outside the self, almost independent of it, to which one can now refer when one's way is lost. This provides the individual with an other-than-self reference against the threat of self-deception. It is not absolute, for even in this, conceivably, he might be deceived. But it functions in life as an absolute; that is the important thing. There is available to the convert a time-space symbol which is for him the moment above all moments in his life—when he met his God in utter encounter. And nothing is ever the same again. He can always come back to it and get perspective and redirection for life. Again and again he may lose his path, may fail in a thousand ways, may betray, deny, or even defame the imperative demand; but it is always there to remind, to judge, to convict, to inspire. In Browning's "Paracelsus" he has his philosopher say, "I am a wanderer . . . so long the city I desired to reach lay hid; . . . but I had seen the city, and one such glance no darkness could obscure."

Important as is the moment of commitment, when deep and total consent is given, it cannot be overemphasized that a new process has been initiated in the life. The commitment itself releases vast creative energies, but these energies must be geared to the specific demands of the new life. They cannot be left to dissipate themselves in ecstasies and exhilaration of spirit. There was great wisdom in this respect in the church of my childhood: once each year there was a "revival," when opportunity was provided for the surrender of the individual life to God. The intimate, personal, private surrender had to be publicly acknowledged and proclaimed. On the basis of this, the new convert was accepted in the church by an accrediting ceremony. But the church did not leave him there. He was turned over to the sponsorship of an older Christian, experienced in the Way. For six to eight weeks there was a weekly prayer service attended only by the new converts and their sponsors. At these services the converts were tutored in the approach to public prayer. Experience was provided in leading prayer services. Careful instruction was given in "lining" a hymn. But particularly, during this period, a convert's daily behavior was under the scrutiny of his sponsor. He was constantly reminded that the old way was no longer open to him. In other words, nurture in the Christian life was another way of providing a time of intensive, deepening experience which gave the new resolve a chance to establish itself as a permanent outlet for the creative energies of God. When this period was over, the individual became a regular member of the beloved community. In other words, given the yielding of the nerve center of consent and the active release of the Spirit of God in a man's life, a radical reorientation became possible. This was indeed assumed to be the essential meaning of the experience of commitment itself.

Despite the fact that I have pinpointed a definite moment of crisis as characteristic of the act of commitment, this is not always the case. The yielding of the center of consent may be a silent, slow development in the life. The transformation may be so gradual that it passes unnoticed until, one day, everything is seen as different. Somewhere along the road a turn has been taken, a turn so simply a part of the landscape that it did not seem like a change in direction at all. A person will notice that some things that used to be difficult are now easier; some that seemed all right are no longer possible. There has been a slow invasion of the Spirit of God that marked no place or time.

But the principle remains the same. When the conditions are met, the experience of inflow follows. In meeting the conditions, the temperament of the individual, the particular religious customs by which his life is nurtured, and the dominant notions of the times will all have a part.

These are not idle words of the prophet: "If with all your heart you truly seek me, you shall surely find me." To the persistent knock at the door there is an answer. We live in a universe that is responsive to an ultimate urgency. The secret is to be able to want one thing, to seek one thing, to organize the resources of one's life around a single end; and slowly, surely, the life becomes one with that end.

Here we are faced with the essence of the discipline. Commitment structures a life, giving it internal and particular order. The total inner landscape becomes altered by a central emphasis. In our discussion up to this point we have assumed that the individual involved in commitment begins with a well-defined sense of self. The assumption may be wrong. It may be that only in the experience of commitment is an authentic sense of self born.

3.

Thus far we have been examining a process or law fundamental to life in general and therefore to organisms in particular. We turn now to explore the meaning of commitment more directly in terms of personality. There are three questions an individual must ask himself, and in his answers he will find the meaning of commitment for himself: Who am I? What do I want? How do I propose to get it?

Let us take these in order. Who am I? It is a commonplace that each of us seems to have many selves. Of the numerous encounters the Master had with individuals, none is more dramatic than his meeting with a certain madman, who stood staring at Him out of eyes that reflected the agonizing turmoil within. From his wrists dangled broken chains. He was regarded by his community as possessed by devils; there were times when he became so violent that, as a measure of collective defense, he was seized and chained to rocks. Even then he could not be restrained when the turbulence within him leaped into muscle, bone, and sinew. The chains burst with the pressure and he would go shrieking through the waste places like a wounded animal. This was the creature who faced the Master. He cried out to be let alone. And with gentleness, tenderness, and vast compassion, soft words issued from the mouth of Jesus: "What is your name? Who are you?" And the whole dam broke, and he cried, "My name is Legion!" He might have said: "This is the pit of my agony. There are so many of me, and they riot in my street. If only I could know who I am —which one is me—then I would be whole again. I would have a center, a self, a rallying point deep within me for all the chaos, until at last the chaos would become order."

Fundamental, then, to any experience of commitment is the yielding of the *real* citadel. It must be said again that the process may be slow and devious. Within us all are so many claims and counterclaims that to honor the true self is not easy.

> *A man may live out all his days*
> *Tensing every nerve to do his best*
> *To find at last a dead goal, a false road.*
> *How may he know?*
> *Is there no guide for man?*
> *No shining light by which his steps are led?*
> *Through all the chaos of his years*
> *He seeks to know.*
> *Some say, "Do this, do that,"*
> *Or, "Give up your goods. Hold nothing back*
> *And free yourself to find your way."*
> *Again, "Commit your way to something good*
> *That makes upon your life the great demand.*

Place upon the altar all hopes and dreams
Leaving no thing untouched, no thing unclaimed."
And yet, no peace . . .
"What more?" I ask with troubled mind.
The answer . . . moving stillness.
And then
The burning stare of the eyes of God
Pierces my inmost core
Beyond my strength, beyond my weakness,
Beyond what I am,
Beyond what I would be
Until my refuge is in Him alone.

"This . . . This above all else I claim," God says.[3]

How does the sense of self come about? What is the psychic mechanism that produces it? We may find a clue in remembering that we become human beings only in human situations. Sociologists have long insisted upon this. We are held and sustained by a primary social unit; it is the family that gives us a deep private sense of belonging. Here we first begin to have our self defined for us. In the family we are initiated into relationship with others, and this relationship, beginning with the family, establishes the ground of our private meanings—meanings which are bestowed upon us. Once accepted by ourselves, they become *our* meaning. The full weight of such a total meaning becomes clarified for us, for instance, when we consider a course of action. The first question we raise about the contemplated act is not apt to be whether it is right or wrong in some abstract sense. No, the question— silently and instinctively asked—is: If I do this thing, what bearing will it have on the binding relationships that give me my sense of worth, of counting in and for something? If what I am about to do will cut me off from those whose very life guarantees my own, then I think long and carefully before I do it. This is true because the human spirit cannot easily abide isolation, being cut off from

[3] From the writer's volume, *The Inward Journey* (New York: Harper & Brothers, 1961).

those whose life sustains it. First in a primary social unit, then ultimately in God, the individual finds the true ground and source of his self-estimate, the basis of his self-respect. This is what sends a man knocking at many doors until at last he finds one—a central door—over which his own name is written. What a man knows himself to be when he sweeps aside all pretensions is what he is in his own heart, but the discovery is the result of the warming encounter with a caring "other." (Another phase of this same insight will be explored in the chapter on reconciliation.)

Sometimes clinical procedures of analysis, when delicately and sensitively carried out, may be of great value in helping the individual to find his core, or an authentic sense of self. Very often the answer comes in response to something that challenges, grips, and lays hold upon him. This is a part of the growing ministry of commitment. It places upon the individual a solitary demand that pulls to one point of focus all the fragments of his life and makes him whole. Again and again, the testimony is that a man did not know he had been fragmented until he became whole. He did not know he was lost until he was found. The miracle of the experience of commitment is that it draws together all the elements of a man from the many regions of the self and gives them back to him in a single whole. In answering the question "Who am I?" he may be able to say only this: "I am not sure who I am, but I have given all of me that I can find to the pursuit of this consuming purpose, and the answer to the question is beginning to make itself known, even to me."

This is one of the things that resulted so often from the impact of the life of Jesus on those whom he encountered. The woman at the well came back into town and said in effect to all and sundry, "Come and see a man who knows me better than I know myself, who has given my life in all its fragments back to me as a single integrated whole." This is infinitely more miraculous than walking on the water or turning water into wine.

There seems to be an instinctive shrinking from this direct and total kind of experience because the possible tyranny of such involvement is frightening. We tend to hesitate to expose ourselves to great and tragic human need or to challenging issues, because we do not want to give up the emotional security of being able to take refuge behind or within some fragment of the self. The only way we can be made whole in commitment is by finding something big enough to demand our all. Something of this sort may be inferred from the traumatic character, mentioned earlier, of the steps leading up to the moment of conversion. There is a stubborn resistance, not merely because of man's fragmented spirit, but also because of the risk involved in yielding the initiative over one's life. A sense of self is achieved, even in its most elementary aspect, by an arduous process. To give even this tenuous hold over ourselves to someone else—though that Someone be God—is apt to seem a betrayal, a giving up, a loss, of the self. Once the nerve center is yielded, we are fearful that we shall be asked to do what in the light of our accepted behavior patterns is out of character for us or far too difficult. The new behavior pattern growing out of the yielding of our central consent is not yet established. There is an uneasy feeling that if we surrender our will to God, what He will require of us may be utter sacrifice.

Jane Steger in *Leaves from a Secret Journal* says that for a long time she was unable to make the great surrender because she was sure that what God would ask of her would be something so overwhelming that she would not have the courage to undertake it. After long internal struggles she was able finally to yield. To her amazement, the most demanding thing that God required of her was to clean out her bureau drawers, make them neat and orderly, and keep them that way. To do this required a major revolution in her personality.

One of the reasons our age is so beset by the behavior of its youth lies in the fact that we have lost the ability to make great demands on them—an ultimate challenge to all their powers. No one likes to be asked to do what he can do too easily; this is the other side of the coin. The glory of any challenge is the fact that it *is* a challenge. We have only contempt, in the end, for the task that requires no real effort.

When I was a boy, the little fellows of my age played a kind of soft ball down on the lower part of the playing field while the big boys played on the big diamond. My sister had a boyfriend who was playing on the big diamond, and I said to one of my chums, "I bet you the next time Willy Williams comes to bat, he'll let me take his place!" So we went up to where they were, and I asked Willy. Of course he knew better than to refuse—when his turn came, he let me take it. What happened I shall never forget. Though I was frightened and could hardly manage the heavy bat, the pitcher threw the ball as hard to me as he did to the big boys. When I turned away after three strikes, there was so much more to me than there had been before. The demand had summoned my fragments into a moment of focus that has influenced me down to the present time.

We turn now to the second question. What do I want? The reply is wholly dependent upon the answer to the first. Of course, ultimately, as far as content is concerned it is defined by what we are committed to. But one must explore the question also in the light of the kind of analysis in which we are engaged. Our decisions are apt to be surface reflections of what other people want of us. The need for a sense of belonging is so acute that we want what others want. The rationale for this must be understood. It is true that for long stretches of time we are apt to be shadows cast by lights that are not our own. So important is it for our emotional security to be included, to be accepted, that it seems a small price to pay, just to stretch ourselves a little out of shape. Experience after experience must flow through us before we get down to the bedrock of our seeking and desiring.

The Master illustrates this with two parables. One has to do with a certain judge and a woman. She came to him seeking a favor, but was refused. Day after day she came back; she haunted him. Wherever he went, she followed after, always making the same request. At last he relaxed and relented, not because he cared about her—not because he had changed his mind—but to be rid of her insistence. She wanted the favor from the very core of her being. She was not to be put off. She knew what she wanted and asked for it.

The other story has to do with a man who had retired for the night, with his family. His neighbor came to borrow food for an unexpected guest who had arrived at his house. He knocked at the door, made known his need, and was told it was too late to be disturbed, even for a neighbor. But he, too, refused to be put off. Finally, with much grumbling and no little hostility, the sleepy householder got up and gave him what he wanted.

The end sought, the want, that persists through all kinds of discouragement and reverses is apt to be what we really desire at the central place of our spirit. There is a contagion in our lives when this happens that bends the will of others in our direction. All around us we see the operation of this principle. Many years ago, when I was on the faculty of Howard University in Washington, D.C., our home was on the university campus. The back yard was enclosed by a high hedge of evergreens. Several little girls joined our daughter in playing there, safe from passing cars. I observed over a period of time that there was one little girl who apparently always knew what the others wanted to play and took it on herself to direct it. Matters developed to a climax one day in general resentment of her domination. Complaints were heard in all the families, including our own. Parents gave their daughters a variety of pep talks. "Remember who you are (or who your father is, or what your grandfather was)—Who does she think she is, pushing everybody around the way she does? Tomorrow when you go back to play, I want you to stand up to her, show her that you're as good as she is," etc. The next day I was standing where I could see them from an upstairs window. For the first half hour, even at that distance, I could feel the tension in the air.

They moved around like little zombies. Then something happened
—I don't know what—all I know is that little 'Betty' took over
once again. The other little girls never knew what they wanted to
play, and Betty always knew what *she* wanted to play. When they
saw the sunlight in her face they dropped their tools and followed
her. This is an elemental contagion of life, singularly powerful
when it comes to goal-seeking.

Some fifty years ago John Dewey wrote a little book on elementary logic, *How We Think*. In his analysis of the art of reflective
thinking he gives the following steps. First, there is a felt difficulty.
There can be no reflective thought aside from some kind of problem. All thought is involved in problem-solving. Then the difficulty has to be located and defined. The problem has to be pinned
down so that we know precisely what it is that we are dealing with.
Then follow suggested solutions. Now that we know what the
problem is, how can it best be solved? At this point the resources
and knowledge of the individual are uncovered in relation to his
need. The richer the resources—the more comprehensive the
knowledge, the more fruitful the suggestions—the more insight is
available for solutions. Sometimes the individual now seeks help.
Here the counselor comes into his own. From the various suggestions a single, sometimes simple suggestion is lifted out and carefully examined as being the most promising among others. If
closer scrutiny reinforces one's initial impression, then the bearing
of the suggestion on the problem is worked out theoretically. If this
holds, then there is the final step—the corroboration in fact or
experience.

The degree to which this is possible within a given time is often
limited by the nature of the problem. By such steps I may locate a
certain street in an unfamiliar city within a few minutes, or a few
hours; but it may take me ten years or a lifetime to discover
whether my solution to the problem of vocation was adequate. It
is a terrible truth that some errors of choice do not show up until
after a life has been lived. "What do you want, really?" Life in-

quires. In getting to the heart of the problem and finding a sound answer, the process is not unlike that outlined above.

Of course the assumption here is that the question takes a concrete form, that it deals with a specific moment of confrontation, and this is no gratuitous assumption. Soon or late, it has to be faced and negotiated. Sometimes it comes upon us with a shocking awareness that we have drifted, without ever thinking seriously about it; that we have no sense of commitment whatsoever. We have lived casually, going from one thing to another with a kind of benign and easy grace. Then, around a turn in the road, some demand is made upon us and we are forced to ask the question: What is it we want, really? When we try to meet it head on we discover, perhaps for the first time, that we have never lived our lives intentionally, and therefore now are unable to do it on demand. When a man faces this question put to him by life, or when he is caught up in the necessity of answering it, or by deliberate intent seeks an answer, he is at once involved in the dynamics of commitment. At such a moment he knows what, in the living of his life, he must be *for* and what he must be *against*.

Finally comes the question: How do I propose to get what I want? Here is involved the whole notion of means, of procedures. All the perils of the preoccupation with self and its fulfillment enter belligerently into the arena to do battle. The more clearly I see my direction, the more discriminating I am able to be about the means of following it. If I feel that time is running out, or that what I need for my journey is threatened by others because of their blindness, selfishness, or greed, then I may find it quite in order to be ruthless in seizing from their stubborn hands what I must have. If they will not give in, then I will take it even if it means destroying them in the process. If this is my outlook, the only morality that binds me is the need to secure that without which my own life is diminished, if not destroyed. If my commitment—which grows out of my answer to the question "What do I want?"—is for me the most important thing in the world, as indeed it may be, I may say to myself: Woe to any man who stands in my way!

If the commitment in itself becomes more important than what I am committed to—or, in other words, if the means become more important than the end—then I am prepared to be quite blind to other consequences. It is possible for a man to make an idol of commitment. We see this not merely in regard to political or social goals or systems such as fascism, communism, or democracy. Such blindness is conceivable even on what we think is the way to the Kingdom of God. A man may be so fierce and unswerving in his commitment to what is clearly to him the Kingdom of God in the world that he does all kinds of violence to his fellows in his pursuit of it. All the tenderness and compassion of his spirit harden, and with grim vigor in his righteous dedication he may easily become a religious bigot. Simply that and nothing more. Such a man *cannot* say with James Lane Allen's hero,

I may not boast with the Apostle that I have fought a good fight, but I can say that I have fought a hard one. The fight will always be hard for any man who undertakes to conquer life with the few and simple weapons I have used and who will accept victory only upon such terms as I have demanded. For be my success small or great, it has been won without wilful wrong of a single human being and without inner compromise or other form of self-abasement. No man can look me in the eyes and say I ever wronged him for my own profit; none may charge that I have smiled on him in order to use him, or called him my friend that I might make him do for me the work of a servant.[4]

There must be a relation between the way I journey to my goal, under the aegis of my commitment to it, and the goal itself. But I must not make the mistake of subjecting the technique of my journeying, or the means of getting to my goal, to a kind of rigor which I refuse to apply to the goal itself. It is entirely possible for a man to answer the question about what he wants in terms essentially unworthy of him. The goal itself must be constantly re-

[4] James Lane Allen, *The Choir Invisible* (New York: Macmillan, 1897), p. 359.

vised and refined. However, one must not let the revision of his goal be determined by the fact that it is hard to achieve. There is apt to be much confusion and frustration when a goal remains remote, and from some points of view it may seem reasonable to decide that because it is remote it is therefore impractical. In such a decision the temptation is to scale down the demands of the goal to the level of the events of one's own life or circumstances.

Indeed, the particular goal may be out of line with a man's possibilities as he sees them, but here he must proceed with great caution; it is possible that what he is committed to may seem, in terms of its empirical implications, so remote in the time of its fulfillment that he will decide he was mistaken. The religious experience of the individual is most important at this point. If, out of a man's fundamental commitment to God, he is led to work on behalf of a fulfillment so high that its full realization is not even in sight, then he must interpret his share as that of participating in a collective destiny as far removed from the present as the divine event itself. Instead of looking forward to a rounded fulfillment or achievement of his goal, he knows that his role is but a part of a larger whole. As the Seeker after Truth says, in Olive Schreiner's *Dreams of the Hunter,*

I have sought; for long years I have labored; but I have not found her. I have not rested, I have not repined, and I have not seen her; now my strength is gone. Where I lie down worn out, other men will stand, young and fresh. By the steps that I have cut they will climb; by the stairs that I have built, they will mount. They will never know the name of the man who made them. At the clumsy work they will laugh; when the stones roll they will curse me. But they will mount, and on my work; they will climb, and by my stair! They will find her, and through me![5]

In answer to the question as to how he will function, a man may decide that his part is minor or humble, yet in line with the

[5] Olive Schreiner, *Dreams* (Aurora, N. Y.: The Roycrofters, 1928), pp. 26-27.

great and audacious outline. The point at which he functions is crucial, and there must be reflected in each tiny thing he does the utter integrity of the whole. The dream to which he is committed must not be betrayed even in the little part he is called upon to perform.

In arrogance a man may be inclined to glory in what he achieves, in what his part is, as compared with what others before him or his contemporaries have done or are doing. But no, he must judge his performance by the goal to which he is committed, not by what others do who seem to have the same commitment. When a man measures his achievement by his goal, the sense of inadequacy makes for an ever-deepening humility and corresponding heightening of concentrated effort. Glenn Dresbach voices this insight in his poem on "Defeat."

> There is defeat where death gives anodyne,
> And all desires of the battle wane
> In deep forgetfulness, and the one slain
> Lies with his face turned toward the firing-line.
> There is defeat where flesh fails the design
> Of Spirit, and the groping, tortured brain
> Sees glories lost it cannot win again
> And wears itself out like effect of wine.
>
> But no defeat is quite so imminent
> To common ways as the defeat Success
> Turns into when it puts aside the dreams
> That made it be, and somehow, grows content
> With what it is, forever giving less
> Until it is not, and no longer seems.[6]

[6] Glenn Ward Dresbach, "Defeat," from *Morning, Noon and Night* (Boston: The Four Seas Company, 1920), p. 39.

GROWING IN WISDOM AND STATURE

GROWTH MEANS DEVELOPMENT IN THE LIFE OF AN ORGANISM. IT means change manifest in structure. In highly developed organisms such as man, growth means change in structure and quality of character. Generally it does not mean random development—an irresponsive or irresponsible change. Perhaps there is no such thing as random development. The term suggests lack of understanding of the process at work in an organism, a lack which causes the development to seem out of line or out of character. This is because inherent in the concept of growth is a certain ordered quality, an orderliness or plan. The lines along which the growth of any particular form of life takes place are fundamental to that form itself. A recent poet to the contrary notwithstanding, Scripture tells us truly: thistles do not grow from figs, nor figs from thistles.

For our purposes here growth means the orderly process of development through which a form of life goes from seed to fruit, from egg to matured animal, from cell to embryo to adult human being. It will be our task to explore some of the ways in which the growth of human beings yields or makes for the kind of discipline in the individual that is essentially spiritual in character. This is not to suggest that it guarantees spiritual experience. But rather, given such development in the life of the individual, he stands an immediate candidate for spiritual experience. Growth provides raw material which can be used in that way. What is taking place at the level of the physical organism may find its counterpart in the life of the mind and spirit.

I.

A part of this has to do with our relation to time. In human life the time interval between two phases of a single experience may be so close as to be without measurement. For the baby, for example, wish and fulfillment are often a single experience, caught and contained almost at a single point in time. Of course for some babies this is not true, depending upon conditions. The mother may not be able to meet a need because of lack of energy or health, too many other pressing demands, or indifference. But ordinarily the observation holds—and particularly for the first baby in the family. When the baby comes, the entire household is reorganized and a new timetable of family activities created. For such a baby the time interval between wish and fulfillment is, in effect, zero.

The baby expresses his wishes in a universal language—crying. It is interesting that for the newborn child this is the language he must speak as the sign that he is *alive*. The family, particularly the mother, becomes adept at interpreting his feelings and needs. In time, she knows what each cry signifies; she recognizes at once whether an outburst is one of anger, pain, frustration, or panic. As soon as the cry is heard, the response is immediate on the basis of interpretation of the felt need. Out of her knowledge and resources as a mother a dry napkin is provided, or food made available, or the baby is taken up and reassured.

But as the baby grows older and is more and more an accepted part of the household, the sure signs of a counterrevoution begin to emerge. The time interval between the baby's cries and the adult response begins to widen. Now, quite properly, the duties of the household, the demands of other children and/or other members of the family, all tend to introduce a kind of delayed action on the part of the mother. The immediate reaction of the child is clear and precise: varying forms of protest from the sustained whisper to the roaring scream (these two words are used together quite advisedly). Sometimes it is a battle of nerves between the baby and the mother.

At this point the baby is having his initial encounter with spiritual discipline. A pattern of life has been interrupted. In the presence of an expanding time interval between wish and fulfillment the child is forced to make adjustment, to make room in the tight circle of his life for something new, different, and therefore threatening. The baby begins to learn how to wait, how to postpone fulfillment. He thus finds his way into community within the family circle.

In the short novel by Carl Ewald called *My Little Boy, My Big Girl*, there is a most instructive discussion of parental reaction to the dual impact of the baby's behavior on his mother and father. The father says, "Often he screams quite horribly which, according to his mother, is a sign of quite remarkable physical and psychological qualities. I ought to be pleased and I am, even if sometimes I do long for the time when he will find more acceptable ways of displaying his prowess." Continuing in the next paragraph he says, "At times his screaming makes me quite unreasonable and I blow up. Then the mother of the wonder rises in all her splendor, repeats what she has already impressed on me a thousand times and asks finally: 'Would you rather he were silent and sickly?' Whereupon I retreat from the battle, silent and beaten."

But there comes a day when the father gets a fresh insight. This is how he expresses it: "He gets fed at regular intervals; but when he has screamed a while . . . he is sometimes picked up and given extra attention. Then as his screaming breaks off in the middle of a wail my suspicion is aroused. Why should a true male give up halfway? Suddenly I stand in the bedroom, tear him away from his mother's tender arms and throw him brutally back into the crib he ought never to have left."[1]

If the response of the parents or others continues to be available on demand, the conscious or unconscious intent being to keep the time interval at zero between wish and fufillment, the baby begins to get a false conditioning about the world and his place in it. For if he grows up expecting and regarding as his due that to wish is to have his wish fulfilled, then he is apt to become a permanent cripple. There are many adults who for various reasons have escaped this essential discipline of their spirit. True, in terms of physical and intellectual development they have continued to grow. Their bodies and minds have moved through all the intervening stages to maturity, but they have remained essentially babies in what they expect of life. They have a distorted conception of their own lives in particular and of life in general.

Consider such a person. Unable to accept himself in relation to the life around him, he uses his creativity and resources to try to jockey the people of his world into becoming creatures responsive to his own wishes, desires, and finally his basic will or intent. He makes his choice of friends from among those who are responsive to his private purposes. The person who does not fit into such a scheme is eliminated or regarded as hostile, or to say the least, unfriendly. When he is blocked or thwarted in his effort, the spiritually immature person reverts to an adult form of the tantrum: "telling them off," "blowing his top," "speaking his mind" so that he will not be regarded as a "pushover." Every possible device is used to bend the other person's will to his own.

On a larger and more tragic scene, this is what happens sometimes when one nation goes to war against another, to make the country attacked the agent of its national fulfillment in the shortest possible time interval. Stripped of all the pretensions of national

[1] Carl Ewald, *My Little Boy, My Big Girl*, Beth Bolling, trans. (New York: Horizon Press, Inc., copyright 1962), pp. 27-28. Used by permission of the publisher.

honor and sovereignty, aggression in war is at bottom an effort on the part of one nation to keep the time interval between its national desires (often confused with national interests) and their realization as close to immediacy as possible. The country that seems to block this procedure is an enemy and must be subjugated. When a man is not able to achieve the desired end by threats or acts of violence, he seeks to achieve it by purchase or through gifts or favors, bartering advantage as best he can. And so nations, too.

Even God may not be exempt from this kind of distortion in the mind and emotions of the believer. This is one of the central problems in prayer, as we shall see. Suffice it to say here that again and again, through importuning, bargaining, and even truculence the individual may seek to enlist God on behalf of his effort to keep the interval between wish and fulfillment close to zero. This element must not be confused with the necessity for genuineness and integrity in the experience of prayer.

The effort to shorten the interval is natural to growth; to know when waiting is essential to the process and to the life of the individual is to be disciplined in one's spirit. To learn how to wait is to discover one of the precious ingredients in the spiritual unfolding of life, the foundation for the human attribute of patience. This is not to imply that patience is always a virtue, always desirable. Sometimes it is merely an escape into inaction because of fear or cowardice or laziness. Sometimes it may be sheer confusion in the presence of a demand that overwhelms and engulfs. What seems to be patience may be a state of inertia, the result of unyielding weariness or exhaustion. As such, it is sterile and lifeless.

But constructive patience as a way of handling the expanding time interval is much more than mere passive endurance. First one has to take a hard and searching look at the environment, particularly at the context in which one is functioning. What is happening? What is responsible for the delay? This is the direct and obvious way to begin the assessment of environmental factors.

Here again, watching the baby may help. For instance, one sees a baby cry and get no response. It seems to make a simple reflex decision to the effect that there is no response because the cry is not loud enough. The baby puts more energy into the cry, increasing the output until it becomes explosive. At times it develops into sheer rage. No response. Now there may follow a period of silence. There is a lurking quality in the quiet, as if the baby were not quite sure of the new situation; as indeed he is not. "Perhaps no one is around and I am alone," one can imagine him thinking. Nevertheless, the waiting is coiled to spring as soon as the slightest sound is heard. Then it happens. He hears voices in the next room or some familiar sound, and the crying starts again.

The same elements are present when the adult is dealing with a similar problem at his own level. He must try to answer the question, "Why is the interval expanding?" Meanwhile he must *wait* it out. In assessing the environment one may discover that the matter of time has been overlooked. The wish, the desire, may be good and worthy in itself, but the timing of its expected fulfillment is off. The wish may be premature in its application to reality. Sometimes a desire can have no significant meaning in a situation because the way has not been prepared for it. The way has to be made ready for fulfillment to honor the wish. This can be seen to best advantage in simple human relations. Your desire is to make another person realize something about himself of which you are sure he is not aware, but which cumulative observation has confirmed in your experience with him. If you are wise and you really want to communicate—that is, if you wish to convey to him what, if he understands it, will mean the fulfillment of your desire, a new realization in himself—then attention must be given to the time and place of your sharing. If you say it at the wrong time, he cannot even *hear* what you are saying. Under such circumstances even the truth becomes error.

I have a friend who has an amusing understanding with his wife, and she with him, covering this contingency in domestic life. If his handerchief is sticking some distance out of his jacket pocket when he comes home from work, she knows it is not his day for being able to handle any ideas or circumstances that require patient understanding and consideration. If she is wearing a certain embroidered apron when he gets home, he knows it is not her day. Each has to postpone the wish-fulfillment of sharing until there is an "opening" in the mind and emotions of the other. Meanwhile, an additional opportunity is provided for testing once again the validity of the desire to share as well as the thing to be shared. Here is an important discipline for the spirit without which good human relations cannot be achieved, however overwhelming may be the desire to speak at once. Here waiting is a virtue!

The value of waiting may be even more active and dynamic in its effect. Sometimes when the wish—the desire—cannot be fulfilled as the individual demands or wants, he may discover that the responsibility involved in its fulfillment would be more than he is capable of handling. It may be that his wish is out of character for the real tenor or quality of his life. It may be something grafted rather superficially on his thought and feeling, which does not really belong there at all. Thus the time of waiting provides an opportunity for revising, refreshing, and reshaping the initial desire.

This is quite strikingly true when desire takes the form of dreams of the mind and heart. "A man has to saddle his dreams before he rides them"—before they come within the wish-fulfillment formula. It is the nature of dreams to run riot; it is difficult to contain them within fixed limits. Sometimes they are the cry of the heart for the boundless and the unexplored, the untried, the unknown. Often they are the offspring of hopes that can never be realized and longings that can never find fulfillment. In such cases, wish and fulfillment seem to be one and the same thing. Sometimes they are the weird stirrings of ghosts of dead places, or the kindling of ashes on a hearth long since deserted.

Many and fancy are the names by which they are called—fantasies, repressed desires, vanities of the spirit, will-o'-the-wisps. Sometimes we dismiss them by labeling their indulgence daydreaming, by which we mean taking flight from the realities of our world and dwelling in the twilight or radiance of vain imaginings.

This may be true. But their meaning need not be exhausted by such a harsh or bitter judgment. The wish in the manifestation of the dream belongs to us. It comes full-blown out of the real world in which we work and hope and carry on. It does not have to be an impostor. It is no foreign element invading our world like some solitary comet from the outer reaches of space, which pays a single visit and is gone, never to come again. No! The dream, the wish is our *thing*. It becomes other when we let it lose its character and its belongingness as it takes flight from its origin in our minds. Here often is the fatal blunder. Our dreams must be saddled with the hard facts of our world and our experiencing before we ride them off to fulfillment among the stars. Thus a dream becomes for us the bearer of a new possibility, the enlarged horizon, the great hope. Even as it romps among the constellations, it comes back to its place in our lives and in its fulfillment reflects the radiance of the far heights, the lofty regions, and gives to our day the lift and magic of the stars!

While the experience of waiting is ours, we discover the meaning of patience and understand the need to assess our lives in terms of our own desires, purposes, dreams, goals. Milton expressed it, and the quotation of his familiar lines will not come amiss:

> *When I consider how my light is spent,*
> *Ere half my days in this dark world and wide,*
> *And that one talent which is death to hide*
> *Lodged with me useless, though my soul more bent*
> *To serve therewith my Maker, and present*
> *My true account, lest He returning chide,*
> *"Doth God exact day-labor, light denied?"*
> *I fondly ask. But patience, to prevent*
> *That murmur, soon replies, "God doth not need*

Either man's work or his own gifts. Who best
Bear his mild yoke, they serve him best. His state
Is kingly. Thousands at his bidding speed
And post o'er land and ocean without rest;
They also serve who only stand and wait."[2]

2.

Growth means the experience of becoming aware of the self as self. Awareness of the self is rooted initially in the experience of the body. I visited one evening with a friend of mine who was baby-sitting with his infant son, asleep in an adjoining room. Presently we heard what seemed to be the beginning of a cry, then a short whimper, and finally sounds of genuine anguish and distress. We investigated. The baby had thrown off all the covers, he was not fully awake, and his big toe was in his mouth and he was chewing it. Even though he had no teeth in evidence, his gums were very firm. The pain he was inflicting on himself made him cry, but he did not know it was his own toe that he was chewing. In fact, he had not become "toe aware." This was one of the first steps in experiencing his own body. To round out this experience is to take one of the primary steps in growth.

How close the relationship is between the growth of the body and of the mind and the spirit we do not know accurately. It was said of Jesus that he increased in wisdom and stature and in favor with God and Man. In the development of the body the experience of standing alone marks one of the watershed moments of personality. Even the person who sees it is caught up in its contagion. For many days and weeks, in the most natural way for a quadruped, the baby moves with his body horizontal, parallel to the floor. His locomotion is by crawling. Then one day something goes on within him that compels him to try for the upright position. Instinctively, he looks around for support. He discovers it in something close at hand but a little higher than his body; it comes down to the level of his eye. He reaches for it and tries to pull

[2] John Milton, "On His Blindness."

himself up. There is a crash as the tablecloth yields to the pull, and once again he is in familiar juxtaposition with the floor, while around him are the broken pieces of his mother's treasured vase.

Of course the child cannot grasp his mother's reaction to his behavior. It must be very puzzling indeed. But he cannot be put off. Another time comes. With a fresh start he finally makes the upright position. Behold him now! There he is, suspended between ceiling and floor with his little feet touching; his entire body shouts, "I did it! I did it!" Then the floor rises up to meet him. But he has established for one prophetic moment his independence of his environment. He has made the crucial physical distinction between the self and the not-self. The meaning of physical distance is experienced. He stands unsupported and alone, an autonomous object in the midst of a world of objects, and there is *room* for movement between them. The peculiar place of the self is established—never quite to be lost again.

The primary experience of the body becomes uniquely personal in standing alone. Within the walls thus established the individual makes his world and builds the fabric of his self-realization. He is now ready to experience his own mind. To discover that thought is private and that there is a world of meanings, feelings and ideas that belong to oneself alone is the clue to man's ability to be creative and to think creatively. The body takes its nourishment, draws its energy, by extracting it from matter. It would seem that this should be the immediate ground for a sense of continuity between the body and objects in the environment. To establish distance between the self and the not-self is therefore reassuring and threatening at one and the same time. But to experience the mind as mind is to be able to establish psychological distance between the self and the not-self in a very different dimension. When this occurs the child encounters the same moment of independence as to mind that standing alone establishes for him at the level of body.

There are implications in the fact that the mind takes its energy neat. It draws nourishment from ideas, meanings, feeling tones, concepts, and the like. These come into the mind disembodied, and must be traced to sources that are tangible and concrete. In time ideas become identified with persons, places, social units. Once this has begun to happen, standing alone becomes an act of defiance, antagonism, self-assertion, or integrity. The long process of re-establishing relations on one's own terms is the great difference between maturity and the lack of maturity. To experience one's own mind is to begin the long journey to discover what, after all, the individual ultimately is.

The initial act of standing alone, of establishing a sense of independence of the environment, is one of the prime requisites for participating meaningfully as a person in a collective destiny that involves more and more of the human family. If man were never able to do this, it would be impossible for him to create and carry his environment with him. This unique ability has made it possible for him to make his home anywhere on the planet, in widely differing circumstances. Control of the environment, and the increasing degree to which this is possible, depend on the making and use of tools, the utilizing of materials given in the surroundings—none of which could be done if in the first instance the graphic distinction between self and not-self had not been achieved. The discipline is not merely in the fact of the achievement, but through it in making the external world an instrument of the private will and the creative mind. The strength to do this comes as a part of the discipline of growth. This is to experience one of the triumphant aspects of growth itself!

3.

Growth also means the experience of crisis. This is a form of tension. In the growing child tension has the same basic elements that are present in the dynamics of crisis wherever found. It is created by two forces making contradictory demands simultaneously. On the one hand there is the push toward the new, the unexplored, the unknown and untried. This is the essential pull of all adventure. It causes the child to "get into trouble" with his environment because he is always upsetting something that is fixed in its place. It makes him try to open all closed doors, pull out bureau drawers, get the feel of fire, experiment with electric outlets—the list is as long as it is hazardous. The restlessness seems to be innate and is not at first geared to specific desire or intent.

I sat in a railway station one day, with a mother and her two little children on the other end of the bench. She was trying to read a newspaper. The children were busy with their particular explorations. First they opened and closed the series of doors to telephone booths; then they examined a drinking fountain to see if they could make it behave as they had seen adults do; they studied various suitcases, turning them over to see if they could get them open; then they saw a writing desk and two chairs, under which they crawled; after that they opened and closed the drawer to the desk. The mother kept saying, "Why can't you keep still and behave?" In exasperation she would get up, find them, give each a quick spanking as she sat them down beside her on the bench. Even as they sat quietly by her for a few minutes, they began exploring the contents of her purse. The urge to explore, the push toward the unknown—this is inherent in the life of the child. It does not seem to be a response to something from without but rather the expression of some deep urge that wells up from within. As someone said, "It is madness to sail an ocean that has never been charted before, to look for a land the existence of which is a question. If Columbus had reflected thus he would never have weighed anchor; but with this madness he discovered a new world."

In a footnote to her discussion on *Women and Labor,* Olive Schreiner tells this allegory. An old mother duck brought her young ducklings down to what had once been a pond. Since her last brood of ducklings, the pond had become nothing but baked mud. But the mother did not realize this. She stood on the bank urging the ducklings to go down, swim around, and disport themselves on the chickweed where there was no water and the chickweed had long since disappeared. While she was doing this, her ducklings with their fresh young instincts smelled the chickweed and heard the water way up above the dam. So they left their mother beside her old pond to go in quest of other water or get lost on the way (this is the risk). They said to her as they left, "Mother, for you and all the generations of your ducklings before us, this may have been good water. But if you and yours would swim again, it must be in other waters."[8]

It should be understood at once that, in responding to the inner urge, there is no *intention* to be destructive, irreverent, or iconoclastic; it is simply a response to a basic urge upon which, in a very large sense, the continuation of life depends. In some curious way it seems to be tied up with what is called the will to live. Sometimes there seems to be an independent entity within the organism that commands it and makes it move upon the environment like an autonomous seeker. The notion here expressed can be seen most clearly in the fable of the yeast cake and the frog sitting side by side on a park bench. Someone inadvertently spilled water on the yeast cake, and it began at once to ferment, with corresponding expansion. The more it expanded, the more it crowded the space available to the frog. At length in desperation the frog protested, "Yeast cake, why don't you stop pushing me, crowding me off the bench?" In dismay the yeast cake replied, "I'm not pushing you, I'm just growing." Nothing deliberate is involved here; the inner urge must be honored. Simply this, and apparently nothing more.

But this is not the whole story of the anatomy of crisis. There is another impulse at work, as authentic as that just noted. It is the inner urge to pull back, to withdraw, to stay put, to *hold*, as it were—an unadmitted, perhaps unconscious intent to conserve, consolidate, hold the line against change and all its sundry implications. The child knows this as a part of his experience of growth.

[8] Olive Schreiner, *Women and Labor* (New York: Stokes, 1911), p. 49.

Often he shrinks from the new, the untried. It seems quite natural to be frightened of the strange or the unfamiliar. The tendency seems more pronounced during certain periods of childhood than in others. At such times, to become identified with the unfamiliar is to be threatened with isolation from the group. To get out of step in dress or language is to be exposed to marked penalties.

When our older daughter was a child, I brought her from Mexico a beautiful Mexican dress and a multicolored belt to wear with it. When she saw it she was quite pleased and excited. But she was unwilling to wear it to school except on occasions when all the other girls were wearing strange clothes as a part of some special project or program. In my unwisdom I felt somewhat let down because she was unwilling to wear it quite normally to school. Here was a perfectly normal tendency at work—the urge to be like all the others, to hold back, not to make a single step down a new road. The risk of isolation was too great. This impulse cannot be completely separated from the felt need to belong, to count in a group, which belongs to another phase of growth and development.

Generally the attitude of holding back is thought to be characteristic of age, definitely of old age. When the sun falls full on the back, instead of in the face, the notion runs, it is important to take refuge in the "fixed idea." And yet this is sometimes far from the case. Two years ago I had dinner with a friend who was in his ninety-fifth year. Despite the obvious lessening of his physical powers, his mind, interests, and enthusiasms were geared to the unexplored areas of life. He told me that during the past year he had read more profoundly and thought more deeply than ever before. At last, he said, the mystery of the second law of thermodynamics was beginning slowly to unfold before his probing mind. And we talked of Tennyson's "Ulysses."

> . . . *You and I are old;*
> *Old age hath yet his honor and his toil.*
> *Death closes all; but something ere the end,*

Some work of noble note, may yet be done,
Not unbecoming men that strove with gods.
The lights begin to twinkle from the rocks:
The long day wanes: the slow moon climbs: the deep
Moans round with many voices. Come, my friends,
'Tis not too late to seek a newer world.
Push off, and sitting well in order smite
The sounding furrows; for my purpose holds
To sail beyond the sunset, and the baths
Of all the western stars, until I die.

Though much is taken, much abides; and though
We are not now that strength which in old days
Moved earth and heaven; that which we are, we are;
One equal temper of heroic hearts,
Made weak by time and fate, but strong in will
To strive, to seek, to find, and not to yield.[4]

The urge to pull back, to refrain from exploring the new is found among the young—and not merely little children who must remain, of necessity, in a tight little world. Much of my life has been spent working on college and university campuses; it is my judgment that on almost any campus the students are apt to be more on the side of holding back, of not upsetting what for them is the familiar pattern, than the faculty. Mark you, I use the word *apt*. This is in large part because students must have something solid and unyielding in the academic climate against which they can exert pressure. There is a profound security in the assurance that there is something that holds despite all pressures exerted against it.

In spite of all the variations and apparent contradictions in the behavior pattern of even a single individual, the tension between the impulse to go forward and the impulse to stay put is a part of every man's experience, young and old alike. When tension between the two impulses reaches a certain degree of strain, the entire inner life is held in precarious balance. Such is the crisis of

---

[4] Alfred Tennyson, "Ulysses."

growth. It is resolved only when one impulse or the other is victorious. Which of them will win, and with what results for the life of the individual—sometimes for the life of a generation, a nation, or an age? The resolution takes place on many fronts and in a variety of ways. The story is never consistent or the same all round. The word growth in this connection has to be modified by the phrase "in this or that respect." Thus a person may say "Yes" to the impulse to push ahead, to explore, in one aspect of his life—but in another he may say "No." In other words, we do not grow in all directions at one time or, perhaps, ever.

Thus this principle of growth is involved even in the resolution of tension. The tension cannot stand indefinitely. It has to be resolved in one way or another. The resolution is in terms of holding back or letting go, of staying put or moving ahead. In fact, it is in terms of change, and this is true even if the decision appears to fall on the side of no movement or no change. For, once the crisis is made plain and the decision taken against change, a different basis for continuing has emerged. The situation is never as it was before the issue was faced or forced.

In its extreme form, the anatomy of crisis is seen in certain illnesses. When I was a boy, typhoid fever was common. The disease moved slowly into the crisis phase marked by a mounting temperature. All kinds of remedies were employed to try to break the fever or precipitate the crisis in a positive way. The time of crisis was the awesome period—children were not permitted to play in the yard; often there were special prayer meetings at the church or in the house. We knew that the duration of the crisis was limited—it had to be resolved one way or the other. If the fever broke, the patient lived; if it did not break—if it held—the patient died.

In the crisis of growth the place of deliberate choice figures importantly in the result. To make a judgment about it requires a kind of deliberation and objectivity which is scarcely possible to the person involved. Such judgment is more possible for an observer; or for the individual concerned, after the fact. Nevertheless, there is an inescapable responsibility for the choice made, even though the impulses at work move at a deeper level in a person's life than may be clearly indicated by deliberate choice. Sometimes the choice seems to be merely a response of the individual to the impact of the environment upon him—simply this and nothing more.

If at the time of crisis there is someone at hand who can interpret the meaning of what is happening on the spot, the maximum good can be garnered for the richness and maturing of the life. The meaning of the experience can be sensed, if not understood, and the efficacy of its discipline embraced, if not comprehended. Many years ago, at the beginning of our work in California, our younger daughter was faced with the most searching crisis of her young life. Twenty-four hours before her mother was scheduled to leave for a two-week trip to Central America to attend an international conference, word was suddenly received that the companion who lived with her grandmother had died. The grandmother lived in a town some fifteen hundred miles away. The question the family faced was: who would go to the distant town to take over the situation until new arrangements could be made for another companion? In the family discussion it was agreed that Mrs. Thurman should go on with her plans to attend the conference, that I should remain on the job in San Francisco, and that our two daughters should go to take care of things until their mother's return.

As soon as the decision was reached, the younger girl got up from the table and ran up the stairs, weeping. I heard her room door close. After a few minutes I went up to see her. I knocked at the door and, when I was admitted, found her stretched out on her bed, sobbing and crying. I sat beside her. After a few minutes I said, "I didn't come up here to urge you to stop crying. I came to explain to you *why* I think you're crying, so that you'll understand what I think this whole experience means to you. You're not crying because you don't want to go away for the rest of the summer and miss the fun with your chums, and so on. You're crying because for the first time in your life the family is asking you to carry your end of the stick as a member of the family. There is something inside of you that knows that when you get on the train tomorrow morning, one part of your life will be behind you forever. You'll never again be quite as carefree and nonresponsible as you were before."

The discipline is in the inescapable responsibility of the act itself—the responsibility for it, and the wisdom this responsibility makes available to the individual. To refuse to choose is, in itself, to make a choice. All our life long we are fashioning a private pattern made up of the resolutions of the crises of growth. Such a pattern gives to each life a dominant trend which becomes an essential—not a casual—part of character.

4.

Growth always involves the risk of failure to fulfill what is implicit in a particular life, its potential. Reference has already been made to the fact that life shows "a precise tendency toward goal-seeking." This is a characteristic expression of all life and is indigenous to it. It is not an invasion from outside. The response of any form of life to the impact of the environment is along the lines of a definite inherent bias. This basic bias or inherent pre-disposition makes leaves shape themselves a certain way, determines the development of flower and fruit, calls a halt to growth in a given time, and establishes the boundaries for each living thing. The bounds are set within. The moving dramatic presentation of this entire concept as applied to all nature is found in God's words in the Book of Job. To select one among many passages:

> *Do you know how wild-goats breed on the hills?*
> *Can you control the calving of the hinds?*
> *Do you fix their appointed time?*
> *Do you know when they are to bear?*

Down they bend, and the womb opens,
and they drop their young—
lusty offspring, thriving in the open,
that run out and return not to the herd.

Who gave the wild-ass his freedom?
Who let the swift ass roam at large,
whose home I make the steppes,
whose dwelling is the salty land?
He scorns the noisy town,
he hears no driver's shout;
he scours the hills for pasture,
in search of any green thing.

JOB 39:1-8 (Moffatt)

Human beings, for reasons only partially understood, are creative and can make choices which help to determine their development, but may prove to be mistaken—that is, may prove to be
self-defeating, or defeating for the particular life. This is one of the
crucial aspects of human freedom. Again and again the individual
is faced with live options.

Wherever a choice is made, error is a possibility. That is, error
in terms of the meaning of the goals of the individual life—not
necessarily error as viewed by some observer, even an interested
and friendly one. This awareness of the possibility of error sometimes paralyzes all action. It is not to be wondered at that men
spend much time and effort to devise means of reducing the
possibilities of error, if not of protecting themselves altogether.
Many there are who fear to make any decision lest it be the wrong
one. I have known at least one man in my life who was convinced
that his predisposition in any decision at all was always on the
side of error. In fact, he said to me, "As I look back on my life,
it seems every basic decision I have ever made was wrong. And my
tragedy is that I was sure at the time that it was wrong, but
couldn't do anything about it. In some curious way I don't think
I'm capable of making a right decision."

The possibility of error is essential to any understanding of the significance of mistakes. The error potential inherent in human life, geared as it is to the finitude of man's existence, is at least one of the major marks of distinction between man and other animals or forms of life. As a creature, he is bound in his body by the tendency inherent in the form of life he represents. His body grows as other bodies grow. The life in him fulfills itself, or works toward that fulfillment, in what we have seen as a tendency to goal-seeking inherent in life even in its simplest forms. But beyond this direction, in his mind, his desires and dreams—man as a child of God—he is capable of living in another realm. He has the face of a man, the body of an animal, and something within him that always wants to fly—to mount upon wings as eagles. Man is more than a creature, he has a mark of the image of God in him; he is a creator of worlds, a dreamer of dreams, and a fashioner of kingdoms. As such, he is involved in a context of relationships which he shares with his fellows, and what he does at any particular moment or in any given circumstance involves others as well as himself. Thus his responsibility for his actions, his choices, is in effect not confined to himself. This fact alone has much to do with the constant threat of error. Though a man make a private or personal choice, its bearing on the lives of others is ever present. Not only is his decision made on the basis of data that are never quite complete as far as what the choice means in his own life is concerned; the data with respect to the lives of others affected by his choice are even less complete, less adequate. Yet the responsibility of the individual can never be isolated or confined to himself alone. "No man is an island."

It is clear that the tendency to goal-seeking reaches its apotheosis in man's mental and moral life. This means that any understanding of what is meant by a mistake, an error, a wrong choice, must extend the notion of responsibility beyond what binds a man to the deed flowing from his decision. It must include his responsibility for *how he deals with the responsibility for his deeds.* True, the possibility of being mistaken, of failing to achieve what the choice appears to indicate, is ever present; nevertheless, failure has to be faced, redeemed if possible, or accepted as a part of discipline in the growth of wisdom and understanding.

A man may be powerless to protect himself from certain impacts that belong to his age, his period, his social or religious heritage, but he is privileged to take these into account as they register in the kind and quality of his choices. This is a great and purging discipline. In the light of these considerations, choices are often made to bring personal relief from external pressures and to serve ends which the individual knows to be less than worthy. If they are made in pique, out of a sense of injury, pain, or guilt, then they may issue in results that stifle growth and positive development. It is enough at this point to say that error may be present because of a false or inadequate reaction to a given set of circumstances. Such an error may defeat a man's dreams, stunt his spirit, and send his highest hopes crashing to the ground.

Never to be forgotten is the fact that the real possibility of failure, deriving from the constant threat of error, is one of the real challenges to growth. To guard against this and be prepared to deal with it when it occurs is an authentic discipline of the spirit. To be victimized by error and at the same time keep on making choices with integrity is to grow in grace. And for the religious man, it is to grow not only in grace but also in the knowledge and experience of God.

There is one more aspect of the problem that must be considered. A man may decide, may elect to do, the thing his insights say to him is against life, or against God. It is possible for the will to become corrupt. Men do sin—all men. Sometimes a man goes against his own sense of values, of right. And this deliberately. Sometimes he does it after weighing the consequences as nearly as he can and deciding on a course of action that is wrong according to his best insight and knowledge. The delight, as he sees it, in taking such a course may outweigh the overt penalty of it. A friend of mine told me that once, when she was a little girl, the circus came to her town. Her parents had forbidden her to stop by the circus grounds on her way home from school. Deliberately she weighed the pros and cons, not in terms of the ethics involved but in terms of the punishment for disobedience. She decided for the circus, feeling that the joy of seeing it would be worth the whipping.

But the problem is not always so simple. Sometimes it takes ten years, twenty years, a lifetime, to determine whether a choice is a bad one. This is not to be wondered at, but the time interval required for the results to come in is sometimes long indeed. Often the involvements are so complex that the erosion in a life, the slow dying of qualities that have scarcely taken root in it, do not manifest themselves until a moment of crisis or special demand.

Oswald McCall has a striking description of this process:

But the other day a piece of rubber that had bound and tired a wheel lay discarded by the road, and, being older now, and aware of what the years can do, I pushed the degenerate stuff with my foot and saw in it the image of a life.

The rubber had the same form as when it was a vital, resilient, and serviceable thing. Nevertheless, it was sapless as sand. It guarded the sad secret well in its dry and juiceless heart, betraying never at all that the soul had gone out of its very proper shape—until I asked it to behave as one has a right to expect rubber to behave. Then I learned.

For I took it and found it would not stretch. It crumbled, broke. It had *perished!*[5]

When a person goes against his values in the choices he makes, the failure is automatic. Here I do not mean that he fails to achieve his ends, for this may not be the case at all. The failure is in the man himself, not in what he is doing—that may or may not follow directly. For instance, when the wrong choice is made in innocence, the external results may follow in terms of ruthless realization of what has been set in motion by the act, but the inner failure is somehow mitigated. There is a kind of immunity in in-

[5] Oswald W. S. McCall, *The Hand of God* (New York: Harper & Brothers, 1957), p. 35.

nocence. In the other instance, when the choice is a deliberate violation, in time there will be guilt, which will becloud the life and bring about chaos and confusion within it. This is what the Master calls the sin unpardonable—the sin against the Holy Spirit. The New Testament incident is very instructive. His friends sought to ease the pressure upon him from his accusers by saying he was a little out of his mind—not insane, but slightly off balance. His accusers said that he was all right as to his mind but possessed by the Devil, and that it was by the power of the Devil that he was casting out devils. Hearing this discussion, Jesus declared that they did not speak with much wisdom. He said that a house divided against itself could not stand. The man who said that he was casting out devils by the power of the Devil was calling a good thing bad, deliberately. To do this is to commit an unpardonable sin because it is a sin against the Spirit of Truth.

A further word must be said about failure where the element of choice seems irrelevant. As has already been implied, failure may be due to forces set in motion beyond the individual's scope of operation or control. They may originate beyond his ken entirely. Such forces may make a man a means to their end without taking him into account at all. In short, a man may fail because he is a victim of circumstances. If he is able to keep on trying, to keep on working at it, the discipline will help him to make one of the great discoveries of the human spirit: that there is sometimes a radical difference between failure and being mistaken or in error in one's choices. There is no harder lesson to learn in the spiritual life than the fact that results belong to God. A man's responsibility is to seek before God how to purge his life of those things that make for error and wrong choices, and to act in the light of his best wisdom and most profound integrity. Beyond this, the results are in God's hands. Of course, a man is never free of the sense of responsibility for results, but this is ultimately a gratuitous concern on his part.

The Master tells the story of a nobleman who prepared to go on a long journey. Before he left he called his three servants, giving them each a twenty-dollar bill and saying, "Trade with this until I come back." When he returned, he ordered them to appear before him for their report.

The first man said, "Sir, your twenty dollars have made one hundred."

"Fine," said the nobleman.

The second man said, "Sir, your twenty dollars have made fifty dollars."

"Excellent," said the nobleman.

The third man was the only one who made a speech. He said, "Sir, here is your twenty dollars. I kept it safe in a napkin, for I was afraid of you. Perhaps you do not know this, but you have a reputation of being a very hard man. You pick up what you have never put down. You reap where you have not sown, you gather into barns what you have not planted!"

The nobleman was incensed. He ordered the servant cast off his place into outer darkness.

The unfortunate servant was not cast out because he failed to realize a profit for his master. No. He was cast out because he did not work at it. We are never under obligation to achieve results. Of course results are important, and it may be that this is the reason effort is put forth. But they are not mandatory. Much energy and effort and many anxious hours are spent in anticipation of the probable failure or success of our ventures. No man likes to fail. But it is important to remember that, under certain circumstances, failure is its own success.

Of course, it is true that implicit in the act itself is a sense of awareness of the probable results of the act. But to keep one's eye too much on results is to distract markedly from the business at hand—that is, to be diverted from the task itself, to be only partially available to its demands. Very often it causes one to betray one's own inner sense of values; for in order to hold fast to the integrity of an act one may have to be willing to arouse, as a by-product, the kind of displeasure which in the end will affect the results. But if the results are left free to form themselves in terms of the quality and character of the act, then all one's resources can be put at the disposal of the act itself.

There are many forces over which the individual can exercise no control whatsoever. A farmer plants a seed in the ground and the seed sprouts and grows. The weather, the winds, the elements, he cannot control. The result is never a sure thing. So what does the farmer do? He plants. Always he plants. Again and again he works at it—in confidence and assurance that, even though his seed may not grow to fruition, seeds do grow and they do come to fruition.

The task of men who work for the Kingdom of God is to *work* for the Kingdom of God. The result beyond this demand is not in their hands. He who keeps his eyes on results cannot give himself wholeheartedly to his task, however simple or complex that task may be.

To summarize: the discipline is to hold steadily before one's life the fact that in all my options as a growing human being I may make the fateful and deliberate choice that will wreck the totality of my striving—I may make the choice in the light of my best judgment, my most lofty insight, and find that in doing it I fail to achieve what I would. There is no known guarantee against the possibility of error. To act with all possible clarity may still prove to be an error. There is a challenging statement from Olive Schreiner's *From Man to Man* that summarizes the idea in graphic terms.

I have sometimes thought it would be a terrible thing if when death came to a man or woman, there stood about his bed, reproaching him, not for his sins, not for his crimes of commission and omission toward his fellow-men, but for the thoughts and the visions that had come to him, and which he, not for the sake of sensuous pleasure or gain, had thrust always into the background, saying "Because of my art, my love and my relations to my fellow-men shall never suffer; there shall be no loaf of bread less baked, no sick left untended, no present human creature's need of me left unsatisfied because of it." And then, when he is dying, they gather round him, the things he might have incarnated and given life to—and would not. All that might have lived, and now must never live for ever, look at him with their large reproachful eyes —his own dead visions reproaching him; "Was it worth it? All the sense of duty you satisfied, the sense of necessity you labored under: should you not have violated it and given us birth?" It has come upon me so vividly sometimes that I have almost leaped out of bed to gain air—that suffocating sense that all his life long a man or a woman might live striving to do his duty and then at the end find it all wrong.[6]

Thus a man is driven back upon one of the most ancient insights of religion: that there is a Purpose that invades all his purposes and a Wisdom that invades all his wisdoms. To seek to relate oneself to such a purpose and such a wisdom is to seek to know God and to walk in His Way. The discipline of growth becomes the discipline of the spirit, and the increase in stature and wisdom can mean a growth in the knowledge of God and the understanding of His Kingdom. Thus the Master teaches us that if we seek the Kingdom and His righteousness, all else will be ours. We will not be guaranteed against failure, but we will learn that we may fail again and again and yet be assured always that we are not mistaken in what we affirm with all our hearts and minds. The prayer of the Psalmist becomes our prayer: "Thou compassest my path and my lying down, and art acquainted with all my ways. For there is not a word in my tongue, but lo, . . . Thou knowest it altogether. . . . Search me, O God . . . try me, and know my thoughts and see if there be any wicked way in me, and lead me in the Way everlasting."

[6] Olive Schreiner, *From Man to Man* (New York: Harper & Brothers, 1927), pp. 458-59.

3

SUFFERING

SUFFERING IS UNIVERSAL FOR MANKIND. THERE IS NO ONE WHO escapes. It makes demands alike upon the wise and the foolish, the literate and the illiterate, the saint and the sinner. Very likely it bears no relationship to the character of the individual; it often cannot be assessed in terms of merit or demerit, reward or punishment. Men have tried to build all kinds of immunities against it. Much of the meaning of all human striving is to be found in the desperate effort of the spirit of man to build effective windbreaks against the storm of pain that sweeps across the human path. Man has explored the natural world around him, the heights and depths of his own creative powers, the cumulative religious experience of the race— all in an effort to find some means of escape, but no escape is to be found. Suffering stalks man, never losing the scent, and soon or late seizes upon him to wreak its devastation.

Prof. Thomas Hayes Proctor of Wellesley College, in an address delivered in Houghton Memorial Chapel in April 1940 commented in this vein:

Men may do much with intelligence and resolute will since Nature is to some extent plastic and may be molded nearer to the heart's desire. But time and tide, disease and death, the spots of the sun and far-off galaxies are not within our power, nor will they be in any future imaginable to man. Nor is there any surety in Nature that the future will be better than the past. It may well be worse. No one who faces fact can deny the possibility of ultimate catastrophe. The values that give dignity and worth to life may be swept away; the causes that we cherish may be defeated, disruptive forces may destroy civilization; in some distant era even human life may become impossible on a cooling planet, and the whole epoch of human living be the briefest of moments between dead eternities. . . . Our deepest loves are at the mercy of a wandering germ.

There is an impersonal quality about all human suffering. It humiliates and violates the person and often the very dignity of the human spirit. It seems to be utterly unmindful of consequences and blind to both good and evil. Nevertheless, there is something utterly personal and private about it; the encounter with suffering is always personal at the point of contact with the individual. An earthquake may destroy a city in a vast upheaval that seems like the temper tantrum of elemental forces. Yet to every human being who suffers loss of family, loss of limb or of life, it is a moment of naked intimacy with pain, terror, and disaster.

The setting for suffering is the world in which we live. Life is hazardous. The Master says that God makes his sun to shine on the evil and the good, his rain to fall on the just and the unjust. In Luke 13 there is a very incisive comment.

It was at this time that some people came to tell him about the Galileans whose blood Pilate had mingled with their sacrifices. But he replied to them,
"Do you think, because they suffered this,
   that these Galileans were worse sinners than the rest of the Galileans?
I tell you, no;
   unless you repent you will all perish as they did.
Or those eighteen men killed by the fall of the tower at Siloam?—
   do you think they were worse offenders than the rest of the residents in Jerusalem?
I tell you, no;
   unless you repent you will all perish as they did."
                                                    LUKE 13:1-5 (Moffatt)

Man's journey is hazardous because the world in which he lives is grounded in order and held intact by an inner and irresistible logic, by laws that, in one vast creative sweep, encompass the infinite variety of the universe and give life its stability, but at the same time make living anywhere, at any time, a dramatic risk for any particular unit of life, be it man or plant. It is on such a stage, in such a setting, that the drama of the private life and the collective enterprises of man is played. Though suffering is a private encounter, and in the last analysis a man must deal with it in solitariness and isolation, it is ultimately reassuring if it can be placed in a frame of reference as universal and comprehensive as life itself.

Suffering is always pain in some form. A thing that is not capable of feeling pain cannot suffer. A simple working definition is that suffering is physical pain or its equivalent, with reference to which the individual may be inspired to protect himself, so that despite its effects he may carry on the functioning of his life. I have deliberately left this statement awkward; I want the basic elements to appear in a simple sentence. Let us examine the component parts.

I.

Suffering is a form of physical pain. It is rooted in pain; where there is no experience of pain, there can be no suffering. Suffering has no meaning outside of consciousness, and further, the potential of the experience itself is co-extensive with life. Pain may be experienced at a level of life that is not capable of interpreting the meaning or fact of the pain. It may be a reflex within an organism where self-consciousness, as such, is diffuse and general. The sense of self may be one with total consciousness, of whatever degree. The more developed the sense of self and the more acute the self-awareness, the more definite is the potential for suffering.

It is reasonable to suppose, then, that so-called subhuman forms of life do not suffer in death to the extent that human beings do. Such a supposition may be entirely erroneous. To hold such a view and to be guided by it in matters of fact is to swing wide the door to all kinds of carnage and misery. Under such circumstances it is easy to inflict pain indiscriminately upon others by the simple device of defining them as subhuman and therefore as nonmembers of the human family.

This is one of the functions of hate during times of war. The enemy nation is defined as comprised of subhuman beasts, brutes, savages; then we are free to inflict pain without a violent pang of conscience. During the war with Japan I saw billboards in California showing Japanese men as monsters with huge grotesque faces, large buck teeth, enlarged black-rimmed glasses—in short, they were not human beings at all. To destroy them would be a righteous, or at least decent, act. In a very penetrating insight, Olive Schreiner suggests that historical Christianity has misunderstood or misinterpreted the teaching of Jesus concerning reverence for life in his insistence that God cares for the sparrow that falls by the wayside, for the grass of the field, the birds of the air, and even the numbering of the hairs of the head. She insists that Christianity as it has developed since the time of its founder wrongly limits the ethical concept of reverence for life to human personality. Once this exception is allowed, the rest is simple. Deny personality to human beings and the ethical demand no longer obtains. Much of the evil in human life and society is rationalized in this way. People who are victimized by injustices must be defined as being, in Kipling's phrase, "the lesser breeds without the law." This makes conscience easy in the face of inflicted pain. When such a definition has social sanction and approval, all kinds of brutality take place as a matter of course and there is no sense of ill-doing.

To illustrate how much a part of the mores such attitudes become: When I was thirteen years old and living in Florida, I worked in the afternoon after school for a wealthy white family in one of the residential areas of our town. During the fall I raked leaves each afternoon. In the family there was a little girl about five years old who delighted in following me around while I worked. She would scatter the leaves as fast as I raked them into a pile. I grew tired of this. I suggested that if she did not stop I would report her behavior to her father, of whom she had marked fear. This so incensed her that she ran over to me, took a pin out of her little pinafore and stuck me on the hand. I drew my hand back and asked her if she had lost her mind. She looked at me in amazement and said, "That didn't hurt you really! You can't feel!"

The same point is demonstrated in the moving account of Carl Ewald in his novel *My Little Boy, My Big Girl*. Let the story speak for itself.

There is great warfare and a lot of noise among the children in the yard.

I hear them yell *Jew*. I go to the window and see my little boy bareheaded out in the front line of the battle.

I settle down quietly to my work again, certain that he will appear shortly and tell me all about it.

Soon after he is there.

He stands next to me, as is his habit, and says nothing. I steal a glance at him—he is highly excited, feels very proud and happy, like one who has fearlessly done his duty.

"Such fun you had down there."

"Well," he says modestly, "—it was only a Jewish boy we were beating up."

I jump up so my chair turns over.

"A Jewish boy—you were beating him up—what had he done?"

"Nothing."

His voice is not very confident, for I look so queer.

But this is only the beginning. For now I grab my hat and run out the door as fast as I can and yell:

"Come on—come on—we must find him and ask his forgiveness."

My little boy hurries after me. He does not understand a word but he is terribly in earnest. We look in the yard, we shout and yell. We rush into the street and around the corner. Breathlessly we ask three people if they have seen a poor, mistreated Jewish boy.

All in vain. The Jewish boy and all the persecutors have vanished.

We sit up in my study again—the laboratory where our soul is crystallized out of the big events in our little life. My brow is knit and I drum with my fingers on the table. The boy has both hands in his pockets and doesn't take his eyes from my face.

"Well—" I say, "there is nothing more we can do. I hope you will meet that boy some day so you can shake hands with him and ask him to forgive you. You must tell him that you did it because you were stupid, that if anyone tries to harm him again, you will help him and beat them as long as you can stir a limb."

I can see from my little boy's face that he is ready to do my will. For he is still a mercenary who does not ask under which flag he serves so long as there is battle and booty. It is up to me to call forth in him the staunch soldier who defends his native land. Thus I continue:

"Let me tell you—the Jews are very wonderful people. You remember David whom Dirty read about in school? He was a Jewish boy. And Jesus whom everybody worships and loves although he died two thousand years ago. He was also Jewish."

My little boy rests his arms on my knees and I go on with my story.

The old Hebrews rise before our eyes with a splendor and power quite different from Dirty's Catechism. They ride on camels in their colorful clothing and with their long beards . . . Moses and Joseph and his brothers and Samson and David and Saul. Wonderful stories these are. The walls of Jericho fall before the blast of the trumpets. . . .

"And what else?" says my little boy, using an expression habitual to him when he was much younger and which still comes to his lips when he is carried away.

We hear of Jerusalem's destruction and how the Jews took their little boys by the hand and wandered from place to place, scorned, despised and mistreated. How they were not allowed to own houses or land but could be only merchants, and how the Christian robbers took all the money they had saved up. How they remained true to their God and maintained their ancient, sacred rituals amongst all the strange peoples who hated and persecuted them.

The day belongs to the Jews.

We look at old books in the bookcase which I am very fond of and which were written by a Jew with a strange name, which my little boy doesn't understand at all. We learn that the most famous man in Denmark at present is a Jew.

And when evening comes and Mother goes to the piano to sing the song that Dad loves best of all it appears that the words were written by one Jew and the melody composed by another.

My little boy is hot and flustered when he goes to sleep that night. Restlessly he tosses in his bed and talks in his sleep.

"He is a bit feverish," his mother says.

"No wonder. Today I vaccinated him against the meanest of all common blights."[1]

Physical pain is fundamental to man's experience as a creature. We do not know why, but we do know that for the most part it serves the function of a signal of danger. If a man could feel no pain, there would be no warning sensation when a particular action becomes self-destructive. Pain is man's first line of defense against death. Pain cannot protect one against it finally, but it may function to trigger a deploying tactic against death. It makes it possible in some instances for a man to have an important part in determining when he shall die. If he uses pain as a warning and seeks to ascertain its cause, he may be able to take measures that will prolong his life and thus postpone the time of his dying. In this sense death may operate on an ascending or descending scale in man's life. The operation of the law of the constant and the variable is applicable here. In response to the alert of pain, a man may approach the control of his own death as the variable approaches the constant. He may narrow the gap, but he can never close it.

In a discussion of physical pain in his book, *The Soul of the White Ant*, the South African Eugene Marais makes the interesting point that, in all of nature, the only experience of pain that is not involved in alerting the organism to danger is the pain of childbirth. He takes the rather obscure position that pain in childbirth is positive and creative because it is the alchemy of the pain that awakens mother love in the female parent. If we accept this thesis in essence, then both aspects of pain have in them elements that are positive and creative.

But this does not exhaust the possibilities of physical pain. Be-

[1] Carl Ewald, *My Little Boy, My Big Girl*, Beth Bolling, trans. (New York: Horizon Press, Inc., copyright 1962), pp. 81-85. Used by permission of the publisher.

yond its warning function as a danger signal it often persists as a reminder that all is not well. The early pain that sends a man to the doctor for examination may lead to the discovery of cancer, but long after such a discovery, if the cancer is not rooted out the pain continues and usually increases with mounting intensity. There is a logic in the pain itself. Whatever else we may say about physical pain, it must be emphasized that what is called pain is a pattern of behavior of cells sensitized by a system of nerves that function out of an integrated center. There is an anatomy of physical pain which is orderly, precise, and definite.

In the appendix of C. S. Lewis' *The Problem of Pain*, there is a note supplied by a medical doctor from his clinical experience. He makes a distinction between the effects of short attacks of severe physical pain and long-continued pain. With the former the effect is of short duration, even though overwhelming while it lasts. When it is over, it is over and done with. With the latter, the alteration in behavior is apt to be more noticeable. Often great strength and resignation are developed in the character, with a corresponding humbling of pride. Sometimes there is an obvious deterioration in character and disposition. The telling point is made that the failures are so few "and the heroes are so many." Long illness often has the effect of wearing down the life to a slow remorseless grind. "The invalid gives up the struggle and drifts helplessly and plaintively into a self-pitying despair. Even so, some, in a similar physical state, will preserve their serenity and selflessness to the end. To see it is a rare but moving experience."

With reference to mental pain, Lewis has this to say:

Mental pain is less dramatic than physical pain, but it is more common and also more hard to bear. The frequent attempt to conceal mental pain increases the burden: it is easier to say "My tooth is aching" than to say "My heart is broken." Yet if the cause is accepted and faced, the conflict will strengthen and purify the character and in time the pain will usually pass. Sometimes, however, it persists and the effect is devastating; if the cause is not faced or not recognised, it produces the dreary state of the chronic neurotic. But some by heroism overcome even chronic mental pain. They often produce brilliant work and strengthen, harden, and sharpen their characters till they become like tempered steel.[2]

2.

We come now to the next part of our definition—I refer to the phrase "or its equivalent." There is a transfer value in the pain experience. Because man has a mind and is in a very profound sense an experiencer of life, pain is something that is seen as happening *to* him. He is *aware* that it is happening to him. He knows that he hurts—it is a very local experience.

Thus for man suffering is possible. For him the physical pain is interpreted; it is at this point that the crucial issue of all suffering arises. What does the pain mean? What is it saying beyond the fact that it hurts? The most elementary answer to simple physical pain is not far to seek. Certain behavior brings certain results. We learn this at an early age. Put your finger on a hot stove and your finger is burned. This is painful, but in a simple sense very understandable. When we raise the question about pain in its more complex dimension, however, it tends more and more to become unanswerable. Here is a person who is afflicted with an incurable disease; he is young, full of promise, the whole world stretches out before him, boundless and unexplored. But he is assaulted, left to spend his days to the end helpless and smitten. After we answer the why of the disease itself (even supposing that we know the cause of it and how the man contracted it), the crucial problem remains untouched. The moral and psychic equivalent to the physical pain must be dealt with. In other words, the practical problem of suffering has to be faced.

It is not surprising that mankind has tried to place the source of evil or pain at a point in time that antedates history, and thus to establish grounds for its existence outside of individual human morality. Man the individual is too finite, too time-space encum-

[2] C. S. Lewis, *The Problem of Pain* (London: Geoffrey Bles, 1940), p. 144.

bered, to bear on his local shoulders the burden of evil. The responsibility has to be placed, yet God must be protected from too direct an involvement, because there must be some source beyond and outside the struggle which can yield perspective and wisdom to those who are caught in it. Here the story of the Garden of Eden meets a critical need in the struggle of Western man. Responsibility has to be placed, or all moral values in existence vanish as "snow upon the desert's dusty face." Adam becomes the figure whose action, personal in character, makes possible an impersonal involvement of all mankind, and in the story the world of nature is actively involved in disintegration and defeat. The creation of man in the first instance is an act of God. The baleful effects of man's behavior can only be countermanded by another act of God, the precipitation of Himself into time through the appearance of Jesus Christ in history. To those who accept such an appearance as authentic, a way is available for redemption from the suffering that the presence of sin or evil produces.

We are now ready to deal with the first and most practical question men raise about suffering. Is the victim being punished for something he has done? In other words, is suffering punitive? It must at once be admitted that there is punitive suffering in the world. There is such a thing as reward and punishment. We are never sure about how the scales are balanced, but one of our oldest racial memories registers the fact that man is responsible for his actions; that is, he is morally responsible. This means that he may or may not be paid in kind for his deeds, but he may be paid in quality or its equivalent. It is a very curious kind of conflict, complication, and involvement.

When I was ten years old, I broke my arm. The doctor put it in splints and a sling. This happened during the summer at the height of the wild grape season and the series of summer picnics. I researched my entire past to see what I had done to merit this kind of misfortune. I did not feel myself capable of doing a deed so monstrous that I deserved that kind of punishment.

So much turns on the interpretation given. Suppose we decide that the young man described earlier, whose future has been cut off by incurable disease, is not being punished; and suppose we decide further that the disease itself is a part of what may be called the structural dependability of nature. Now what? He is still cut off from his dreams and from all the promise of his life. In other words, he is a sufferer.

Such a man has to handle his suffering or be handled by it. This brings me to the other part of the definition. The mind may work out an immunity so that the spirit of the person not only remains undefeated but is triumphant over his suffering. By "mind" I do not refer merely to the process of stimulus and response, of action and reaction, but mean to include here the individual's total sense of being: the comprehensive focal unity of the man's personality, inclusive of what he thinks and feels. I mean the is-ness of personality. It is this central conscious ground of personal being that is at last confronted by suffering, and in that ultimate private encounter the battle is won or lost.

The suffering may be capitulated to before the issue is so closely drawn. For instance, it may be accepted quite simply, with some disappointment but with resignation, as "one of those things," "I got a bad break," or "it was fun while it lasted." In my high school class there was an extremely beautiful and gifted girl who contracted a fatal illness. The last time I saw her we discussed the whole matter of her imminent death. She said, "I'll tell you, Howard, how I feel about it. I feel as I did when I was a very little girl and went to a play at church with my mother, and we had to go home before the play was over."

There may be hostility directed against life in the abstract; such hostility may embitter the spirit, make the individual wreak his vengeance on all and sundry. Since life is spoiled for him, he proceeds to try to spoil it for others. The people who pay the greatest price are those who are bound to him in ties of ministry and kinship from which there is no easy way of escape. The embittered person says in effect, "I'm stuck with it, but I don't have to like it," or "It's a dirty trick life has pulled and I've got to even the score any way I can—and you're elected."

But if the person comes to grips with his suffering by bringing to bear upon it all the powers of his mind and spirit, he moves at once into a vast but solitary arena. It is here that he faces the authentic adversary. He looks into the depth of the abyss of life and raises the ultimate question about the meaning of existence. He comes face to face with whatever is his conception of ultimate authority, his God.

The first thing his reflection brings to mind is that there is a fellowship of suffering as well as a community of sufferers. It is true that suffering tends to isolate the individual, to create a wall even within the privacy that imprisons him, to overwhelm him with self-preoccupation. It makes his spirit miserable in the literal sense of that word. Initially, it stops all outward flow of life and makes a virtue of the necessity for turning inward. Indeed, one of the ground rules of man's struggle with pain is the focusing of the energies of life at a single point. All of him that can be summoned is marshaled. This is true whether he is dealing with sheer physical pain or the more complex aspects of other dimensions of suffering. The pain gives his mind something else to think about and requires what approximates total attention.

One of the great preachers of another generation tells the story of a stagecoach driver who made a round trip each day between two towns. On a certain morning, halfway along, the lead horse was frightened by a large piece of paper in the middle of the road. It was all the driver could do to keep the team from running away. On the return trip he noticed at some distance the same piece of paper. Now he prepared himself. As soon as the lead horse saw the white object, his ears stood up; as he neared it, his body tensed in fear. At the crucial moment the driver flicked him on the tender part of his ear with his whip to avert a repetition of the event of the morning. The driver gave the horse something else to think about.

Thus suffering may at times seem an end in itself for generating energy in the spirit, as indeed it does. If the pain is great enough to lay siege to life and threaten it with destruction, a demand is made upon all one's resources. In this kind of concentration of spirit, the same thing operates as we observed in the chapter on commitment. The energy of life becomes available when the conditions of single-mindedness are met. It is important to hold in mind that this is the way of life—when life is attacked, it tends to rally all its forces to the defense.

In the case of human life, its forces include not only physical but spiritual resources as well. This is why very often we see people as profoundly changed by their suffering. Into their faces has come a subtle radiance and a settled serenity; into their relationships a vital generosity that opens the sealed doors of the heart in all who are encountered along the way. Such people look out upon life with quiet eyes. Openings are made in a life by suffering that are not made in any other way. Serious questions are raised and primary answers come forth. Insights are reached concerning aspects of life that were hidden and obscure before the assault.

The question remains, however, "Why is this not the experience of every sufferer?" Frankly, I do not know the answer. As already suggested, for some all resources seem to be cut off completely and the withering of the spirit keeps pace with the disintegration of the body or anguish of the emotions. There are all kinds of problems and paradoxes here. Sometimes a person who has always been generous becomes tight and hard under suffering. There are those who before the visitation have had an active religious faith and a vital Christian enthusiasm, but now become dour in spirit and withdraw themselves from all previous religious convictions. These are what the French mystic, Simone Weil, refers to as "the afflicted."

I once knew such a man. All his life he had been an active teacher of religion at two colleges. Generations of students had been helped and inspired both by his example and by the wisdom of his counseling. His children were led to pursue worthy and creative goals in their lives and regarded him as the major anchor in all their journeying on the high seas of their vocational undertakings. Yet there came a time when, in his encounter with personal suffering, he seemed stripped of every resource. His prayer life became increasingly barren; none of the things that had nourished him all through the years could reach him now. All the tides flowed out and the shoals and rocks of his coast line stood exposed in a stark and ugly pattern. Yes, suffering may have this result. For such a time, for such a person, the only thing is to wait it out, to affirm with avid recollection and present insistence that the contradictions of life are never final. All contradictions are held together in an almighty synthesis that gives them, ultimately, a meaning and a context.

As to the demand upon resources created by suffering, let us examine more closely those that become available when the real issues are faced. I have referred to the fact that the individual enters a fellowship of suffering and the community of sufferers. This is obvious and need not be labored. The only point to be held steadily in mind is that, despite the personal character of suffering, the sufferer can work his way through to community. This does not make his pain less, but it does make it inclusive of many other people. Sometimes he discovers through the ministry of his own burden a larger comprehension of his fellows, of whose presence he becomes aware in his darkness. They are companions along the way. The significance of this cannot be ignored or passed over. It is one of the consolations offered by the Christian religion in the centrality of the position given to the cross and to the suffering of Jesus Christ. The theological insistence is that the love of God manifests itself in his son, Jesus Christ. The position is summarized in a telling fashion by Leslie Paul.

God did not just "appear" as a spirit in the fashion of a man, and speak to men out of the visible form to which they are accustomed so that they might not be too astonished or frightened. No, the Son of God *became* a man. He took on the burdens and cares of human exist-

ence. He became a party to human limitations. He suffered in Himself
what it was to be creaturely man. Yes, and much, much more. He en-
dured His human limitations in the greatest pain and loneliness and
encountered human company at its most vile, tasting the spittle of
the rabble on His lips. For the truths that He spoke, the sick that
He healed, and for His very Divinity itself He was taken and done
to death. We do not face only the simple, radiant, joyous revelation
of God to man—would to heaven that we did! We have to reckon
also with the most bitter humiliation, the very deepest human tragedy
—that the Son of God was nailed on a cross by the men He had come
to meet and to save.

Even if one were to call it all a myth born in the unconscious, and
breathe again with relief that man had only imagined this dreadful
deed, and that it had not occurred under the floodlights of day after all
—one would still not be exonerated. For that man should invent this,
out of nowhere—or out of nowhere in his outer world—out of, only,
his deep, inner torment would itself be a cry almost too fearful to
bear from man's soul, a cry telling of man's agonizing need to be redeemed from himself and to find God.[3]

For many Christians the sense of the presence of the suffering
Christ, who in their thought is also the suffering God, makes it
possible through His fellowship to abide their own suffering of
whatever kind or character. To know Him in the fellowship of
His suffering is to be transformed by the glory of His life, and
for these individuals this is enough—in His name they can stand
anything that life can do to them. This is the resource and the discipline that comes to their rescue under the siege of pain.

3.

If the sufferer is merely an innocent victim, what then? One of
the characters in Margaret Kennedy's novel *The Feast* suggests
that the entire human race is tolerated for its innocent minority.
There is a strange and awful vitality in the suffering of the innocent. It does not fall within any usual category. The mind moves

[3] Leslie Paul, *The Meaning of Human Existence* (London: Faber and Faber,
1949), p. 235.

very easily with the balance of the swinging pendulum; we are accustomed to equating things in terms of equilibrium. Our values are defined most easily as merit and demerit, reward and punishment. There is great reassurance for the spirit in the idea that reverses can somehow be balanced by the deeds that have brought them about. Many men are at peace with their suffering when they remember that the pain is deserved, is payment for a just and honest debt. Of course there may be a full measure, pressed down and overflowing, but the hard core of the pain is for acknowledged wrong done; the essence of the hardship is atonement for evil. All this falls into a simple pattern of checks and balances, of sowing and reaping, of planting and harvesting.

But where the pain is undeserved, where innocence prevails and no case can be made that will give a sound basis for the experience of agony, then the mind spins in a crazy circle. Always there must be an answer, some clue must be found to the mystery of the suffering of the innocent. It is not enough to say that the fathers have eaten sour grapes and the chidren's teeth are set on edge. This is not enough. It is not enough to say that the individual sufferer is a victim of circumstances over which he has no control. There is truth in such descriptions, but the heart of the issue remains untouched. The innocent do suffer; this is the experience of man.

Margaret Kennedy's idea is an arresting one. It is that mankind is protected and sustained by undeserved suffering—that swinging out beyond the logic of antecedent and consequence, of sowing and reaping, there is another power, another force, supplementing and restoring the ravages wrought in human life by punishment and reward. The innocent ones are always present when the payment falls due—they are not heroes or saints, they are not conscious burden-bearers of the sins and transgressions of men. They are the innocent—always there. Their presence in the world is a stabilizing factor, a precious ingredient maintaining the delicate balance that prevents humanity from plunging into the abyss. It is not surpising that in all the religions of mankind there is ever at work the movement to have the word *made* flesh, without being *of* the flesh. It is humanity's way of affirming that the innocent *hold*, while the evil men do exacts its due. "Their shoulders hold the sky suspended. They stand, and earth's foundations stay."

But what of those who have no such orientation and whose lives are not girded by such a faith—there would be no problem if suffering came only to those who had, even latently, such a re-source. Are these others abandoned by God and left to languish without a witness of His love, concern, and care, or must they take time out from suffering to find the way into such assurance? One may truly say of many lives that, when they were able to burst out of the prison house of their pain, they found God in the midst of their adversity. But what of the others?

In the first place, when a man is driven by suffering to make the most fundamental inquiries concerning the meaning of life, he has to assess and re-assess his total experience. It may be that he has never seriously thought about the meaning behind the energy of a simple act. He has never thought seriously about God. He has taken his life and all life for granted. Now under the assault of pain he is led to wonder about the mystery of life. Why do men suffer, he asks himself. He sorts out the answers available to him, some of which we have touched upon. He may conclude, perhaps, that suffering is given; it is a part of the life contract that every living thing signs at the entrance. Therefore it must belong in and to life. It is no invasion from the outside. It is no strange phenomenon wandering at random among the children of men. And if it belongs, then it has to be accepted as a part of one's ac-ceptance of life. To reject it is to reject life. This is the first thing that he pins down in his assessment.

If suffering belongs, then does it go along for the ride, or must it carry its end of the stick? Does it have a function? What would life be like if there were no suffering, no pain? The startling dis-covery is made that if there were no suffering there would be no

freedom. Men could make no mistakes, consciously or uncon-
sciously. The race could make no mistakes. There would be no
error. There would be no possibility of choice at any point, or in
any sense whatsoever. It is irrelevant to suggest that there might
be a more satisfactory way to guarantee this than to make human
misery in some sense mandatory. Freedom therefore cannot be
separated from suffering. This, then, may be one of the ways in
which suffering pays for its ride.

The ultimate logic of suffering, of course, lies in the fact of
death. The particular quality of death is to be found in what it
says about the future. Death is a denial of the validity of the future. This is the logic of all suffering. It is what rallies the spirit
and girds man to do battle. Suffering is the gauntlet that death
throws down in the arena. All religions, since man began his
pilgrimage on the planet, have been forced to deal with this
central issue: they must answer the challenge of the end of man's
life. Stripped of all cultural accretions and special limitations of
specific historic situations, religion—regarded as fundamental to
the human enterprise—says that life and death take place in a
larger context, which religion calls Life. Life and death are the
experience of living things, and here Life in some sense becomes
identical with God. To say that man's spirit is driven to deal with
the issue of death is equivalent to saying that man is driven to a
face-to-face encounter with Life and its Creator, out of whom
come life and death as experiences in Life. Death is seen as being
an experience *within* Life, not happening *to* Life.

Why do men suffer? They suffer as a part of the experience of
freedom. They suffer as a part of the growth of life itself. They
suffer as a part of life. This leaves many questions unanswered:
the pain of the innocent, the frustration of wasting illness of one
kind or another. But at last we have a clue in the notion that without suffering there is no freedom for man, and that through it
every man is faced with the necessity of experiencing in his being
—not merely in his physical body—the meaning of death.

How does this happen? It may be said that the experience of death is for every man, as long as he lives, vicarious. It is a highly speculative experience so long as he is alive. But it is embodied in the reality of the world of which he is a part. All around him he sees his fellows die, sees them fail, finally, to continue as he knows them. If suffering is the logic, the intention, *of* this failure, then he knows that for him and all his kind there is a common fate. Strangely enough, it is the profound rejection of his verdict that is absolutely binding. He recognizes that death, through its part in defining duration, does establish a form or aspect of life, and in so doing gives life a meaning and a purpose. It provides a measuring rod for values to be worked out within a particular time interval. If he could settle for this kind of finality, then with death as an established boundary he would be sure that whatever meaning he is to know, whatever fulfillment he is to participate in, must be achieved between the time of his birth and the time of his death. This would enormously simplify life; it would dwarf all experience and make effective a ceiling to all endeavor. The only problem would be of possible miscalculation as to the length of a man's days. But that would be a calculated risk to be taken into account as a rider to all his strivings.

Yet this is not a true picture, for man is aware of desires, of aspirations, of projections that cannot be telescoped into his solitary life span, but are personal nevertheless. Somehow they must be contained in what he means when he considers his life. Desperate, he must establish some kind of finality to existence, some phase of man's life capable of containing not only his time-bound dreams but also capable of containing *him. He* must be dealt with in the equation—not merely his hopes, dreams, and aspirations. There must be an answer that confirms him, that establishes for him a basis of ultimate self-validation. This, religion insists, is found only in God. Always his God must be more than his thought about God, more than his private needs, demands, or requirements. His God must be comprehensive enough to include the whole movement of life in its every dimension and outreach. Man must be able to deal not merely with the fact of death, but also with the fact of life. He must be so confirmed in his living that he encompasses the fact of his dying.

Of course, the classic Christian reference is to Jesus of Nazareth. But there are others before and after him: Socrates, Galileo, John Brown, and others of our own time "who have dared for a high cause to suffer, resist, fight—if need be, to die."[4]

To be confirmed in life is to make even of death a little thing. It is to be robbed of the fear of living and consequently to be robbed of the fear of dying.

This answer to suffering is best seen when men act in response to love. It is only for love of someone or something that a man knows that, because of the confirmation of life in him, he can make death an instrument in the hands of life. Last summer in a town just outside of Edinburgh, a seventy-year-old man was standing on a bridge when he saw a three-year-old child fall into the water. He dove from the bridge, saved the child, but lost his own life. The problem comes home to each of us when we ask ourselves: Under what circumstances and for whom would you give up your life?

I believe that such confirmation of life in us is the work of the Holy Spirit of God. For me, the love of God nourishes and confirms us and gives to us the assurance that, because life in all its vicissitudes is contained in Him, in Him we have the sense of ultimate finality in existence that makes total existence, and our life in it, purposeful and meaningful. I cannot escape the necessity of concluding that the answer to suffering is to be found in experiencing in one's being the meaning of death. To state it categorically, it is to have one's innermost self or persona assured that the finality of death, which is the logic of all suffering, is itself contained in a more comprehensive finality of God Himself. Such a

[4] W. W. Story, "Io Victus," from *Masterpieces of Religious Verse*, James D. Morrison, ed. (New York: Harper & Brothers, 1948), p. 288.

God is conceived as the Creator of Life and the living substance, the Creator of existence itself and of all the time-and-space manifestations thereof. Within the construct of this creation, He is at work pervading it with the quality of Himself. This means that, at any point in human history, no event in the life of a single person can be separated from what are, in fact, the ends of God.

This makes all formal concepts of the problem of evil, all metaphysical questions about evil, merely academic. The problem of evil is literal fact. Evil itself is specific and concrete. But what a man who is suffering wants to know is, "How may my suffering be managed or overcome? Is there any resource available that can reduce it to a unit of containment? Must I finally be overcome and destroyed by it?" The answer is to be found in the testimony of the human spirit. It is not to be found in the books or the philosophies or even in the ritual or ceremonies of religion. All of these may be helpful to the individual in sustaining him against the ravages of his experience. But the man who suffers must say yea or nay, in his utterance feeling himself sustained, supported, and confirmed, or undermined, deserted and denied. If the answer to his suffering is to face it and challenge it to do its worst because he knows that when it has exhausted itself it has only touched the outer walls of his dwelling place, this can only come to pass because he has found something big enough to contain all violences and violations—he has found that his life is rooted in a God who cares for him and cultivates his spirit, whose purpose is to bring to heel all the untutored, recalcitrant expressions of life. Such a man knows that he cannot determine what may befall him, either as a child of nature, as a child of his time and age, or even as a child of God. He knows that suffering, the ultimate logic of which is death in life, is a part of the living stuff of his earthly adventure. He knows that even in his own strength he never quite explores the limits of his endurance, and beyond all this there is the possibility of a reinforcement of his life that transcends all the vicissitudes of his fortune and shares in a collective destiny in which

God is all and in all. Wherever there is such a possibility, to miss it would be to have all sense of the future cut off and all the meaning of even the simplest values of his life disintegrate in his hands. To seek to know how he may enter into such a grand fulfillment is the essence of all wisdom and the meaning of all human striving. Of course, he may be mistaken. But to be mistaken in such a grand and illumined undertaking is to go down to his grave with a shout.

> *Heir of the Kingdom 'neath the skies,*
> *Often he falls, yet falls to rise;*
> *Stunned, bleeding, beaten back,*
> *Holding still to the upward track,*
> *Playing his part in Creation's plan—*
> *God-like in image, this is man.*[5]

---

[5] Source unknown.

4

PRAYER

IT WAS THE YEAR OF HALLEY'S COMET. I WAS A LITTLE BOY LIVING
in a sawmill town in Florida. I had not seen the comet in the sky
because my mother made me go to bed with the setting of the sun.
Some of my friends who were more privileged had tried to convey
to me their impression of the awe-inspiring spectacle. And I heard
my stepfather say one day when he came home for lunch that a
man had been down at the mill office selling what he called "comet
pills." The theory was that if these pills were taken according to
directions, when the tail of the comet struck the earth the individual would be immune. As I remember it, the owner of the sawmill
made several purchases, not only for himself and family, but for
his key workmen—the idea being that after the debacle he would
be able to start business over again.

One night I was awakened by my mother, who asked if I would
like to see the comet. I got up, dressed quickly, and went out with
her into the back yard. There I saw in the heavens the awesome
tail of the comet and stood transfixed. With deep anxiety I asked,
without taking my eyes off it, "What will happen to us when that
thing falls out of the sky?" There was a long silence during which
I felt the gentle pressure of her fingers on my shoulders; then I
looked into her face and saw what I had seen on another occasion,

86

when without knocking I had rushed into her room and found her in prayer. At last she said, "Nothing will happen to us, Howard. God will take care of us." In that moment something was touched and kindled in me, a quiet reassurance that has never quite deserted me. As I look back on it, what I sensed then was the fact that what stirred in me was one with what created and controlled the comet. It was this inarticulate awareness that silenced my fear and stilled my panic.

Here at once is the primary ground and basis of man's experience of prayer. I am calling it, for the purpose of this discussion, the "givenness of God" as expressed in the hunger of the heart. This is native to personality, and when it becomes part of a man's conscious focus it is prayer at its best and highest. It is the movement of the heart of a man toward God; a movement that in a sense is within God—God in the heart sharing its life with God the Creator of all Life. The hunger itself is God, calling to God. It is fundamental to my thought that God is the Creator of Life, the Creator of the living substance, the Creator of existence, and as such expresses Himself through life. This is the meaning, essentially, of the notion that life is alive and that this is a living universe. Man himself cannot be an exception to this fact.

It has always seemed curious to me that man should investigate the external world, recognize its order, and make certain generalizations about its behavior which he calls laws; that he should study his own organism and discover there a kind of orderliness of inner behavior, which he seeks to correct when it acts out of character by a wide variety of ministrations, from drugs and surgery to hypnosis and faith—and yet that he should be inclined, at the same time, to regard himself as an entity apart from all the rest of creation, including his body. Man is body, but more than body; mind, but more than mind; feelings, but more than feelings. Man is total; moreover, he is spirit. Therefore it is not surprising that in man's spirit should be found the crucial nexus that connects him with the Creator of Life, the Spirit of the living God. The apostle is utterly realistic when he says that in Him we live and move and have our being. The most natural thing in the world for man, then, would be to keep open the lines of communication between him and the Source of his life, out of which he comes and into which (it is my faith) he goes.

Prayer is a form of communication between God and man and man and God. It is of the essence of communication between persons that they shall talk with each other from the same basic agenda. Wherever this is not done, communication tends to break down. If, however, an atmosphere of trust can be maintained, then one learns how to wait and be still. It is instructive to examine the prayer life of the Master from this point of view. I am always impressed by the fact that it is recorded that the only thing that the disciples asked Jesus to teach them how to do was to pray. The references are many to His own constant dependence on prayer:

when Jesus had been baptized and was praying, heaven opened and the holy Spirit descended in bodily form like a dove upon him (LUKE 3:21).

In the early morning, long before daylight, he got up and went away out to a lonely spot (MARK 1:35).

after saying good-bye to them, he went up the hill to pray (MARK 6:46).

and he took the five loaves and the two fish, and looking up to heaven he blessed them (MARK 6:41; MATT. 14:19. Cf. MARK 8:6, 14:22; MATT. 26:26; LUKE 24:30).

large crowds gathered to hear him . . . while he kept in lonely places and prayed (LUKE 5:15, 16).

This filled them with fury, and they discussed what they could do to Jesus. It was in these days that he went off to the hillside to pray. He spent the whole night in prayer to God (LUKE 6:11, 12).

Now it happened that while he was praying by himself, his disciples were beside him. So he inquired of them, "Who do the crowds say that I am?" (LUKE 9:18).

he took Peter, John, and James, and went up the hillside to pray. While he was praying, the appearance of his face altered and his dress turned dazzling white. . . . Now Peter and his companions had been over-powered with sleep, but on waking up they saw his glory (LUKE 9:28, 29, 32).

The seventy came back with joy. . . . He said to them, "Yes, I watched Satan fall from heaven like a flash of lightning." . . . I praise thee, Father, Lord of heaven and earth" (LUKE 10:17, 18, 21).

"Simon, Simon, Satan has claimed the right to sift you all like wheat, but I have prayed that your own faith may not fail" (LUKE 22:31, 32).

Then he went outside and made his way to the Hill of Olives, as he was accustomed. The disciples followed him, and when he reached the spot he said to them, "Pray that you may not slip into temptation." He withdrew about a stone's throw and knelt in prayer, saying, "Father, if it pleases thee, take this cup away from me. But thy will, not mine, be done" (LUKE 22:39-42).

Jesus gave a loud cry, "My God, my God, why forsake me?" (Ps. 22:1; MARK 15:34.

Then with a loud cry Jesus said, "Father, I trust my spirit to thy hands" (Ps. 31:5; LUKE 23:46).

To Jesus, God breathed through all that is: the sparrow overcome by sudden death in its flight; the lily blossoming on the rocky hill-side; the grass of the field and the clouds, light and burdenless or weighted down with unshed waters; the madman in chains or wandering among the barren rocks in the wastelands; the little baby in his mother's arms; the strutting insolence of the Roman Legion, the brazen queries of the tax collector; the children at play or old men quibbling in the market place; the august Sanhedrin fighting for its life amidst the arrogances of empire; the whisper of those who had forgotten Jerusalem, the great voiced utterance of the prophets who remembered—to Jesus, God breathed through all that is.

To Jesus, God was Creator of life and the living substance, the Living Stream upon which all things moved, the Mind containing time, space, and all their multitudinous offspring. And beyond all these, He was Friend and Father. The time most precious for the Master was at close of day. This was the time for the long breath, when all the fragments left by the commonplace, all the little hurts and big aches, came to rest; when the mind could be freed of the immediate demand, and voices that had been stilled by the long day's work could once more be heard; when there could be the deep sharing of innermost secrets and the laying bare of heart and mind—yes, the time most precious for him was at close of day.

But there were other times: "A great while before day," says the Book—the night was long and wearisome because the day had been full of jabbing annoyances; the high resolve of some winged moment had spent itself, no longer sure, no longer free, and then vanished as if it had never been; the need, the utter urgency was for some fresh assurance, the healing touch of a heavenly wing—"a great while before day" he found his way to the quiet place in the hills. And prayed.

2.

The Master was always concerned about his Father's agenda. In reflecting on the discipline of prayer, I asked myself how I may find a clue to God's purposes in the world? How may I sense Him at work? Already I am aware of Him in the hunger of my heart; this is a crucial clue. In the depths of my own spirit, then, I may be aware of His Presence, share His Mind, and establish true communication because my will comes to rest in His Will. We shall return to this later in the discussion.

The work of God in the world is another important clue to His agenda. If I can understand this, a rapport is established between God and me which becomes the prelude to communion or communication in prayer. This is what the Psalmist is talking about when he says,

The heavens declare the glory of God;
   and the firmament sheweth his handywork.
Day unto day uttereth speech,
   and night unto night sheweth knowledge.
There is no speech nor language,
   where their voice is not heard.
Their line is gone out through all the earth,
   and their words to the end of the world.
In them hath he set a tabernacle for the sun,
   Which is as a bridegroom coming out of his chamber,
   and rejoiceth as a strong man to run a race.
His going forth is from the end of the heaven,
   and his circuit unto the ends of it:
   and there is nothing hid from the heat thereof.

The law of the Lord is perfect, converting the soul:
   the testimony of the Lord is sure, making wise the simple.
The statutes of the Lord are right, rejoicing the heart:
   the commandment of the Lord is pure, enlightening the eyes.
The fear of the Lord is clean, enduring for ever:
   the judgments of the Lord are true and righteous altogether.
More to be desired are they than gold, yea, than much fine gold:
   sweeter also than honey and the honeycomb.
Moreover by them is thy servant warned:
   and in keeping of them there is great reward.
Who can understand his errors? Cleanse thou me
   from secret faults.
Keep back thy servant also from presumptuous sins;
   let them not have dominion over me:
   then shall I be upright,
   and I shall be innocent from the great transgression.
Let the words of my mouth, and the meditation of my heart,
   be acceptable in thy sight,
O Lord, my strength, and my redeemer.

PSALM 19

Or when he bursts forth:

O Lord our Lord,
   how excellent is thy name in all the earth!
   who hast set thy glory above the heavens.

Out of the mouth of babes and sucklings has thou ordained strength
    because of thine enemies,
        that thou mightest still the enemy and the avenger.
When I consider thy heavens, the work of thy fingers,
        the moon and the stars, which thou hast ordained;
What is man, that thou art mindful of him?
        and the son of man, that thou visitest him?
For thou hast made him a little lower than the angels,
        and hast crowned him with glory and honour.
Thou madest him to have dominion over the works of thy hands;
        thou hast put all things under his feet:
All sheep and oxen,
        yea, and the beasts of the field;
The fowl of the air, and the fish of the sea,
        and whatsoever passeth through the paths of the seas.
O Lord our Lord, how excellent is thy name in all the earth!

                                                          PSALM 8

Any close examination of the world of nature reveals that everything is painstakingly structured. In its functioning, nature operates
on the basis of a rather definite agenda. All animals and plants live
intentional lives. We cannot dismiss this fact by saying that it is
blind instinct or merely a pattern of conformity on the basis of
which the continuity of the particular species is guaranteed. Here
the activity of an innate order is at work. When I am able to read
the specifications, then I can understand the behavior. The same
thing is at work in me as elsewhere in the whole process. This is
why so much knowledge about our own bodies is secured from the
study of other forms of life. Such study is mandatory for all who
would acquire a working knowledge of the human organism. If I
regard this understanding as a part of God's—the Creator's—working paper, then I relate to it not only with my mind but also with
my feelings. I react to what I observe: this is the Hand of God
fashioning His creation. Such a mood of reverence has a transfer
value for me also. It moves me directly into the experience of what
Schweitzer calls "reverence for life." But there is much in familiar-
ity with technology (which is the pragmatic application of a knowl-

edge of the behavior of particles) that stifles any mood of reverence. So rapid and astounding have been our developments in this area that there is little time for the element of reverence to emerge. I doubt very seriously if a scientist who knew reverence as a part of his own response to what his investigation of nature revealed could ever bring himself to the fashioning of atomic or hydrogen bombs.

Now, the mood of reverence opens up the spirit to a receptivity of the greatness of God at work in the world of nature. It heightens one's sensitivity to meaningful overtones of beauty that enliven the spirit and enrich the awareness of values. Here, then, is one important clue to the divine agenda or working paper. Harmony becomes a language the understanding of which opens up a whole world of communication between God and me.

"The universe is not dead. Therefore, there is an Intelligence there, and it is all-pervading. At least one purpose, possibly the major purpose, of that Intelligence is the achievement of universal harmony.

"Striving in the right direction for Peace (Harmony), therefore, as well as the achievement of it, is the result of accord with that Intelligence.

"It is desirable to effect that accord.

"The human race, then, is not alone in the universe. Though I am cut off from human beings, I am not alone.

"For untold ages man has felt an awareness of that Intelligence. Belief in it is the one point where all religions agree. It has been called by many names. Many call it God."[1]

There is an element of profound truth in the outlook of pantheism, which sees the work of God in the world of nature with such clarity as to identify God with His world; the temptation is hard to resist. But this is not enough. God must never be a prisoner in His creation. When I look carefully at my own body, I see at once that my body functions are so closely meshed and integrated that, under ordinary circumstances, I am not aware of any part of my body as such unless the inner harmony breaks down at the point of

[1] Richard E. Byrd, *Alone* (New York: Putnam, 1938), p. 183.

function. I do not become little-finger-aware unless my little finger no longer functions as a little finger should. When the harmony is broken, I say that the part is ill or the body is ill. The body is quite literally a dwelling place of the Most High God, Creator of the Universe. The mood of reverence applies here with telling effect upon man's whole world of values, meaning, and morality.

Further, I seek a clue to God's working paper, His agenda in the world of men, in the whole story of man's collective or social life on the planet. At first look, human relations as experienced in human history, or in the immediate social environment in which we live, seem quite chaotic. The casual view discovers no valid intent; if there be an intent, it seems more evil than good, more diabolical than benevolent. In the language of faith, the kingdoms of this world often conflict with the Kingdom of God. It cannot be denied that a part of the fact of human society is the will to destroy, to lay waste, and to spend. There is often so much that casts down and so little that uplifts and inspires. The bloody carnage of fratricide is a part of the sorry human tale. And yet always, against this, something struggles. Man does not ever quite make the madness total. Always there is some voice that rises up against what is destructive, calling attention to an alternative, another way. It is a matter of more than passing significance that the racial memory as embodied in the myths of creation, as well as in the dream of prophet and seer, points ever to the intent to community as the purpose of life. This is no mere incident of social evolution, or growth toward civilization from times more primitive. It goes to the very heart of all human striving. It is basic to the aspirations of the entire human race. The dramatic character of this phenomenon can be seen during periods of the greatest violence among men —in war. In the midst of the vast death-dealing moments of war between nations there are always voices speaking out for peace. They are not tolerated; they are taken out of circulation so that their spirit may not become contagious; but they always appear and reappear.

Occasionally there comes into view on the horizon of the age a solitary figure who, in his life, anticipates the harmony of which he speaks. No one dreamed that Mahatma Gandhi would be able to introduce into the very center of a great modern empire such as Britain a principle contrary to empire, and abide. For Gandhi to have come out of the womb of a religion outside the Christian faith and address himself to an empire whose roots were nurtured by that faith is the most eloquent testimony of the timeless, universal character of what was working in him. It is as though there were at work in this little man an Intent by which he was caught up, and of which in some way he became the living embodiment. The moving finger of God in human history points ever in the same direction. There must be community. Always, in the collective conscience and in the private will, this intent appears and reappears like some fleeting ghost. It is a fact that mankind fails again and again, but the sense of not being mistaken in the fundamental intention never deserts the final purpose, or the judgment that is passed upon all social behavior.

When the hunger in a man's heart merges with what seems to be the fundamental intent of life, communion with God the Creator of Life is not only possible but urgent. The hunger of the heart, which is a part of the givenness of God, becomes one with the givenness of God as expressed in the world of nature and in human history. It must be pointed out that this hunger may function merely at the level of human striving and enlightened social concern. In this sense it may be regarded simply as a characteristic of personality; only this and nothing more. In other words, it may not become personal in terms of the devotional response of the individual to Life. Or, it may be a clue to the Father's house, to the Holy of Holies, wherein the Creator of Life and the King of the Universe has His dwelling place. Prayer is the means by which this clue is pursued. The hunger cannot be separated from God. For many this is what makes any communication between God and man possible. This is the swinging door that no man can shut. This is not to say that the great God of Life is reduced to or squeezed into the hunger of the heart of man, but that the hunger is an expression of the givenness of God. I repeat: it is the trysting place where the God and the soul of man meet, where they stand on a common ground and the wall or partition between them has no status. It is what Eckhart calls the "apex of the soul—the uncreated element in the soul of man." This is the citadel of encounter.

The true purpose of all spiritual disciplines is to clear away whatever may block our awareness of that which is God in us. The aim is to get rid of whatever may so distract the mind and encumber the life that we function without this awareness, or as if it were not possible. It must be constantly remembered that this hunger may be driven into disguise, may take a wide variety of twisted forms; but it never disappears—it cannot. Prayer is the experience of the individual as he seeks to make the hunger dominant and controlling in his life. It has to move more and more to the central place until it becomes a conscious and deliberate activity of the spirit. When the hunger becomes the core of the individual's consciousness, what was a sporadic act of turning toward God becomes the very climate of the soul.

3.

It will be in order to suggest certain simple aids to this end. One of these is the practice of silence, or quiet. As a child I was accustomed to spend many hours alone in my rowboat, fishing along the river, when there was no sound save the lapping of the waves against the boat. There were times when it seemed as if the earth and the river and the sky and I were one beat of the same pulse. It was a time of watching and waiting for what I did not know—yet I always knew. There would come a moment when beyond the single pulse beat there was a sense of Presence which seemed always to speak to me. My response to the sense of Presence always had the quality of personal communion. There was no voice. There was no image. There was no vision. There was God.

Many years after, I was invited to speak at a Friends First Day Meeting in Pennsylvania. I decided to put aside my usual procedures of preparation for an address and expose myself completely and utterly to the time of "centering down" in the Quaker meeting. I felt that if I were able to share profoundly in that clarifying, centering process the word to be spoken would be clear and sure. I was accustomed to quiet and silence in private but not as part of a collective experience, and I entered into it with some trepidation. After a while all the outer edges of my mind and spirit began to move towards the center. As a matter of fact, the movement seemed to me to be actually fluid and flowing. After some time, I am not sure precisely when, the sense of the movement of my spirit disappeared and a great living stillness engulfed me. And then a strange thing happened. There came into my mind, as if on a screen, first a single word and then more words, until there was in my mind's eye an entire sentence from the Sermon on the Mount. The curious thing was that, familiar as I was with the passage, one part of my mind waited for each word to appear as the sentence built, while another part knew what the sentence was going to say. When it was all there, with avidity my mind seized upon it. I began thinking about it as the text of what I would say. When I was ready to speak, I placed my hands on the railing in front of me and was about to stand, when from behind came the voice of a lady quoting that passage. When she finished, all through the meeting individuals spoke to this theme, and I began to wonder whether I would have a chance to say anything, knowing I had traveled nine hundred miles to do it. At length I had my opportunity to speak.

Silence is of many kinds. There is a silence which is the prelude to prayer—the moment of hush and ingathering. There is a silence that tends to quiet the soundless words that fall from the tongue and to calm the noises of the mind and spirit. Every person who is concerned about the discipline of prayer must find the ministry of silence in accordance with his particular needs. Certain mechanical devices are helpful. We must seek a physical place of withdrawal, a place of retreat, if this is possible. It may be achieved merely by closing the door as a signal that one wishes to be alone; it may be by remaining in bed for a spell after everyone else is up and about; it may be by taking a walk or by extending a walk beyond the initial requirement or demand; it may be by withdrawing one's participation in conversation, even though one has to remain in the midst of company.

Once the physical silencing has been achieved, then the real work must begin. The calming of the mind as an effort to exclude distraction is a complex necessity. The soundless voices take the form of thoughts that distract. One of the most helpful things to do is to read or recall some stilling passage or thing—words that place before the mind a picture or a feeling tone that quiets or subdues and settles. The Psalms are very helpful here. "The Lord is my shepherd, I shall not want." Or, "Lord, Thou hast been our dwelling place in all generations." Or, "Lord, Thou hast searched me and known me." There are many. One may find helpful the literature of devotion aside from the Bible; sometimes a great poem of remembered radiance or a picture which speaks peace to the spirit at a time of great upheaval. Often there is a person whose life gives forth a quality of tranquility as one who has come through troubled seas into a place of calm and confidence.

He understood what it is that we are trying to work out.
He was very old, and from the secret swing of planets
To the secret decencies in human hearts, he understood.
I used to watch him watering his lawn, scattering the food for the
  woodpecker,
Sweeping the crossing before his house. It was not that there was light
About him, visible to the eye, as in the old paintings.
Rather, an influence came from him in little breaths.
When we were with him we became other.
He saw us all as if we were that which we dreamed ourselves.
He saw the town already clothed on for its Tomorrow,
He saw the world, beating like a heart, beating like a heart.

"How may I, too, know?" I wanted to cry to him. Instead
I only said: "And how is it with you?" But he answered
Both questions by the look in his eyes. For he had come to quietness.
He had come to the place where sun and moon meet
And where the spaces of the heavens open their doors.
He was understanding and love and the silence.
He was the voice of these, as he fed the woodpecker.[2]

For many Christians the contemplation of Jesus Christ is the
most helpful aid. I know a man who always, at this point in his
preparations, selects some incident in which Jesus is expressing his
love for someone. He moves into identification, sometimes with the
Master himself, sometimes with the object of the Master's love.

It may be that some problem is so central in thought and concern that it pushes everything else aside. If this happens to be the
case, it should not cause undue distress as regards the business at
hand. The problem itself may clear away everything else and in a
sense perform an important task. This is one of the real services
that an overriding problem may render the life of the spirit. It
clears the decks for action. If such be the situation, then the individual can attack the problem itself as something that deadens the
hunger; thus that which threatens is included in the process itself.
If the problem is considered in the light of what it does to the
hunger for God, this alone will put it into a different context and
a new perspective. It will no longer be regarded merely as something that annoys, frustrates, or discourages, but rather as something that stands squarely in the way, blocking the pathway to
God. Under such circumstances fresh insight is apt to come, and
even if there is no immediate solution one is now in a position to
challenge the integrity of the problem by raising his sights—looking at it from the other side, from the point of view of what it
obscures.

Once the interference that drowns out the hunger has been

[2] Zona Gale, "The Sky-Goer," from *The Le Gallienne Book of English and
American Poetry*, Richard Le Gallienne, ed. (New York: Garden City Books,
1935), p. 293. Used by permission of the author's estate.

stilled or removed, real communion between man and God can begin. Slowly the hunger begins to stir until it moves inside the individual's self-consciousness, and the sense of the very Presence of God becomes manifest. The words that are uttered, if there be words, may be halting and poor; they may have to do with some deep and searching need of which the individual now becomes acutely aware; it may be a sin that had become so much a part of the landscape of the soul that the soul itself has the feeling of corruption—but this may not last long. On the other hand, it may be a rather swift outpouring of a concern, because here is the moment of complete understanding and the freedom it inspires.

Several years ago I was talking with a very old lady about prayer, and particularly her own experience in prayer. She told me a story from her own most recent past. In her little Congregational church in a small New England community there was an extended crisis over the minister. The congregation felt he should leave because his usefulness was over. He prayed about the matter and as a result was convinced that, all evidence to the contrary notwithstanding, he should remain at his post. My friend said that she decided to take the matter directly to God in her prayer time. I quote her.

"I gave myself plenty of time. I went into a thorough review of the highlights of the sixty years I have been a member of the church right up to the present situation. I talked it through very carefully. It was so good to talk freely and to know that the feelings and the thoughts behind the words were being understood. When I finished I said, 'Now Father, these are the facts as best I can state them. Take them and do the best you can. I have no suggestions to make."

A fresh meaning flooded the words 'Thy Will be done.'

The experience of communion may elicit an expression of concern for someone whose need is great or for whom one has compelling love. Such a person may be ill, or in trouble, or in deep quandary before the exacting demands of fateful decision. To bring him and his need clearly to mind, or into complete focus, and expose him tenderly to the scrutiny and love of God through our own thought is to pray for him. At such a moment questions as to the efficacy of intercessory prayer becomes merely academic. I share my concern with God and leave the rest to Him. Does such a sharing do any good? Does it make a difference? The conviction of the praying person is that it does some good, that it does make a difference. Can you prove it, he may be asked. In what does proof of such a thing consist? The question of the effectiveness of intercessory prayer does not belong in the experience of the man who prays for his friend—it is his care that is poured out when he is most conscious of being cared for himself. When the hunger for God becomes articulate in a man so that it is one with his initial experience of God, it is the most natural thing in the world to share whatever his concerns may be. A man prays for loved ones because he has to, not merely because his prayer may accomplish something beyond this.

There is no attempt here to deal with the problems and issues that center in a discussion of what is called intercessory prayer. With reference to these I permit myself one comment only. The man who shares his concern for others with God in prayer does two things at the same time. He exposes the need of the other person to his total life and resources, making it possible for new insights of helpfulness and creativity to emerge in him. In other words he sees more clearly how to relate himself to the other person's need. In the second place, he may quicken the spirit of his friend to a sudden upsurging of the hunger for God, with the result that he is in the way of help from the vast creative energies of God. How this is done we may speculate but never explain. That it happens again and again in the religious experience of the race is a part of the data of the prayer experience itself.

Communion may be an overflowing of utter praise, adoration, and celebration. The sense of awe becomes trumpet-tongued, and the sheer joy of the beauty of holiness overwhelms the mind and enlivens all the emotions with a kindling of spiritual fervor. It is at such a moment that one feels he was created to praise God and to enjoy Him forever.

The communion may be an overflowing of thanksgiving. Here I do not mean an order of thanks for services rendered or for good received. Here is no perfunctory grace before meals, when a person chooses to mumble gratitude either out of habit, or superstition, or because of spiritual breeding of a high order. No, I do not mean this sort of thing, but rather the overflowing of the heart as an act of grace toward God. The overflow is not merely because of what has taken place in life or in the world or because of all the manifestations of benevolence that have covered a life. Something far more profound is at work. It is akin to adoration; it is the sheer joy in thanksgiving that God is God and the soul is privileged and blessed with the overwhelming consciousness of this. It is the kind of thanksgiving that sings itself to the Lord because He is God. This praiseful thanksgiving overshadows any bill of particulars, even though many particular things crowd into mind. We can get some notion of what is meant here when, under some circumstances, we encounter a person who, for what seems to be a swirling temporary moment, enjoys *us*—not what we say or what we are doing or what we represent, but who reaches into the core of our being and touches us purely. How such moments must rejoice the heart of God! I agree most heartily with Rufus Jones when he says that prayer at its best is when the soul enjoys God and prays out of sheer love of Him.

There is one remaining crucial element that must be taken into account in the experience of communion. I refer here specifically to the sense of sin, of unworthiness, that often takes on a dramatic character in the experience with God. Here I am not thinking primarily of human nature and man's general frailty, but more precisely of those awarenesses of having denied the hunger and, in the denial, having done violence to the integrity of the soul and to the sense of goodness and righteousness which became manifest along our journey. This goes deeper than the guilt one feels for going counter to a convention. That may be included, but I refer now specifically to the residue that remains as a man's own deep, personal, and private sense of sin and guilt. Sin has to be absorbed and the guilt washed from the spirit. How this is done we do not know. There are Christians who experience the redeeming love of Christ, which sets them free of guilt because they believe that in some miraculous way He takes their guilt upon Him and absorbs in His Body and Spirit the virus of their sins. For those who believe, the offering of Christ is made to God on their behalf, and in Christ's name they pass from darkness into light.

For many others this whole experience involves something more than can be managed with the mind. There is a strange necessity in the human spirit that a man deal with his sin before God. This necessity is honored in prayer when the deed is laid bare and the guilt acknowledged. I do not know how it happens or quite how to describe it, but I do know that again and again man has come away from prayer freed of his guilt, and with his sin forgiven; he then has a sense of being totally understood, completely dealt with, thoroughly experienced, and utterly healed. This is not to suggest that after the experience a man is always through with his sin. No, but now a solvent is at work on it which dissolves it, and the virus begins to be checked in its breeding place.

The experience of prayer, as I have been describing it, can be nurtured and cultivated. It can create a climate in which a man's life moves and functions. Indeed, it may become a way of living for the individual. It is ever possible that the time may come when a man carries such an atmosphere around with him and gives its quality to all that he does and communicates its spirit to all who cross his path. This was the most remarkable impact of the life of the Master upon those whom he encountered. It was this that stilled the ragings of the madman, that called little children to Him, that made sinners know that their sins were forgiven. His whole countenance glowed with the glory of the Father. And the secret? "A great while before day, he withdrew to a solitary place and prayed, *as was his custom.*"

5

RECONCILIATION

THE LITERAL FACT OF THE UNDERLYING UNITY OF LIFE SEEMS TO be established beyond doubt. It manifests itself in the basic structural patterns of nature and provides the precious clue to the investigation and interpretation of the external world of man. At any point in time and space one may come upon the door that opens into the central place where the building blocks of existence are always being manufactured. True, man has not been able to decipher all the codes in their highly complex variations, but he is ever on the scent.

If life has been fashioned out of a fundamental unity and ground, and if it has developed within such a structure, then it is not to be wondered at that the interest in and concern for wholeness should be part of the conscious intent of life, more basic than any particular conscious tendency toward fragmentation. Every expression of life is trying to experience itself. For a form of life to experience itself it must actualize its own unique potential. In so doing it experiences in miniature the fundamental unity out of which it comes.

The purpose of this chapter is to explore the meaning of man's elemental grounding in unity for the larger life of his mind and spirit as he relates to his fellows. Our immediate purpose is to explore the possibilities in terms of the discipline of reconciliation. It applies not only to ruptured human relations but also to disharmony within oneself created by inner conflict. The quality of reconciliation is that of wholeness; it seeks to effect and further harmonious relations in a totally comprehensive climate.

The concern for reconciliation finds expression in the simple human desire to understand others and to be understood by others. These are the building blocks of the society of man, the precious ingredients without which man's life is a nightmare and the future of his life on the planet doomed. Every man wants to be cared for, to be sustained by the assurance that he shares in the watchful and thoughtful attention of others—not merely or necessarily others in general but others in particular. He wants to know that—however vast and impersonal all life about him may seem, however hard may be the stretch of road on which he is journeying—he is not alone, but the object of another's concern and caring; wants to know this in an awareness sufficient to hold him against ultimate fear and panic. It is precisely at this point of awareness that life becomes personal and the individual a person. Through it he gets some intimation of what, after all, he finally amounts to, and the way is cleared for him to experience his own spirit.

The need to be cared for is essential to the furtherance and maintenance of life in health. This is how life is nourished. The simpler the form of life, the simpler the terms of caring. It does seem to me at times that, even with the simplest forms of life in plants, a new quality of growth appears if, beyond the care expressed in watering and feeding, an additional something is added. One year, in addition to watering my flowers and digging around the roots and so on, two or three times a week I would go into the garden and look at them, brood over them gently, and on occasion verbalize my feelings by talking to them directly. It may have been my imagination, but I am convinced that it made a great difference in the richness of their growth and bloom.

There is less uncertainty about what happens when this need is honored in animal life. A news item appeared not long ago in a daily paper describing a novel kind of job held by a high school girl in a large general hospital. She was employed as a mouse-petter. Her sole occupation was to take the white mice out of their cages several times during each day, pet them, croon over them, and gentle them. It had been discovered that mice treated in this way responded to various experiments with less tension and therefore with more relaxation—i.e., more positively—than those that had not been thus dealt with. The petting touched something deep within them and their response was both automatic and authentic. Their organism was given a sense of well-being that put them at their ease. This enabled them to hold their own against limited upheaval in their environment without panic. The literature growing out of such experimentation with animals is increasingly abundant.

It is in human life that the need to be cared for can be most clearly observed, however, because here it can be most clearly felt. There was a lady in my church in San Francisco who felt very poignantly the need to be needed beyond the limits of her family. One day she went with a small group to visit the children's ward in a hospital. She noticed a baby in a crib against the wall. Despite the things that were going on in the ward and the excitement created by a group of English bell-ringers and their tunes, this little child remained lying on his side with his face to the wall. But it was discovered that he was not asleep—his eyes were open in an unseeing stare. The nurse explained that the entire ward was worried because the child responded to nothing. Feeding had to be forced. "Even if he cried all the time, that would be something to work with. But there is nothing. And he is not sick as far as anything clinical can be determined. He will surely die unless something is done." Then the lady decided to try to do something. Every day for several weeks she visited the ward, took the little boy in her arms, talked to him, hummed little melodies and lullabies, and did all the spontaneous things that many years ago she had done with her own son. For a long time there was absolutely no response. One day when she lifted the child into her arms there was a slight movement of the body, and the eyes appeared to be somewhat in focus. This was the beginning. Finally, on a later day, as her voice was heard greeting the nurse when she came into the ward, the child turned over, faced the ward, and tried to raise himself to a sitting position. Things happened rapidly thereafter until he was restored to health.

When the need to be cared for is dishonored, threatened, or undetermined, then the individual cannot experience his own self as a unity and his life may become deeply fragmented and splintered. In its extreme form the disturbance upsets the balance of the mind, and a man gradually loses his sense of identity. When I was a boy I had a graphic experience of the meaning of this. In the corner down at the end of our street, my mother noticed that a large group of people had gathered and others were coming. She sent me down there to see what was going on. As I got to the corner I saw that the center of attraction was the strange behavior of Kenchion Butler, who ran a barbershop. He was describing a large circle around an oak tree. Each time he completed the circle he would strike the tree with a huge cross-tie ax he had in his hands, and call someone's name. He was clearly out of his mind. The sheriff had come to take him away to jail as a preliminary to sending him to the mental hospital—or, as we said at the time, the asylum. The sheriff could not get to him because of the ax in his hand. It was a game of waiting it out.

Then someone thought of Ma Walker, and I was sent for her. She was a most unusual woman in our community, distinguished for two things: her personal care for all kinds of people, and her beautiful rose garden, dedicated to God. From her garden came roses for the altar table in the church and for funerals. I went to her house, told her the story, and she came back with me. When she was within earshot of the group she called the name of the man with the tortured mind. There was just a slight hesitation in his step as he located her and the sound of the voice, but he kept walking. Meanwhile, she and I approached; the sheriff took his pistol out of the holster and the crowd moved completely to one side, making way for us. I dropped back when we were at the outer edge of the group. Ma Walker kept on, repeating his name as she stood in his circular path. Then they met, their eyes held, she said simply, "Come, Kenchion, you must go home with me." And he did.

Here was a woman who had the quality of personality that could make the gift of reconciliation to another human being. Sometimes it heals the inner breach by the simple offering. What it does is to introduce harmony into another's life by sensing and honoring the need to be cared for and therefore understood. This is the miracle. One person, standing in his own place, penetrates deeply into the life of another in a manner that makes possible an ingathering within that other life, and thus the wildness is gentled out of a personality at war with itself.

The talent of reconciliation may be native to the personality of him who has it—I do not know. But I am confining my thoughts, to begin with, to the inner reconciliation that an individual experiences when he feels that his life is bottomed by another's caring. The roots of such an actively healing disposition may lie in the fact that a person is so profoundly assured that he is cared for that his spontaneous attitude toward others carries over the spirit of this caring. Indeed, he may be so sensitized to the personality needs of others that his self-giving to them is an expression of the natural flow of his life to others in distress. Or he may be so conscious of the way in which the inner harmony of his life is held by another that he feels ever the urge to seek ways of doing this precise thing in the lives of his fellows. Or, out of the assurance that his experience with God confirms and keeps him whole, despite the intruding disillusionments of life, he expresses his praise of God in sharing this quality with others.

In addition to all this there must be a discipline either to develop the talent or to keep it alive. And in what does such a discipline consist? In the first place, there must be the *intent* itself.

The individual must want to do it. A climate must be generated out of which the talent or gift moves forth into the life of another. Such a climate is a matter of growth. It may begin with simple interest in others, a simple identification with them in their need, anguish, or distress. Out of such identification a real searching for ways of approach arises—for keys that will unlock the door to others' lives or for a kind of personal activity in relatedness that may inspire another person to open the door, to turn toward one. In other words, the whole process must be worked at and all personal resources drawn upon to this end. The mood that induces trust has to be developed and projected.

When I took my dog, Kropotkin, to a kennel to be trained, I was very much impressed with the approach of the trainer. I told him what I wanted the dog to learn and why. After listening carefully he said, "I've been working with dogs in training for more than fifteen years. Over this period of time I've developed an over-all attitude toward dogs in general and toward any dog I am to train in particular. Now, any time I see a dog, of whatever kind or condition, at once he is enveloped by a sense of 'dogness' that gathers him to me. I know that my attitude-feeling for him can be trusted. But it takes me from seven to fourteen days of contact to discover if a responding something can come from the dog to me. Once that has happened, the rest is easy and simple. My attitude gentles the dog into trust and confidence. I've had only one real failure in the last five years."

It is essential to the Christian's vocation that attention be given to training in the direction of trust and confidence. Of course, I think such training should enter into every man's vocation, but it is especially binding upon the Christian who undertakes by commitment and intention to follow the teaching of his Master. There is the intent, the desire, the decision—all must become central in the individual's awareness of what he means by himself.

At the Primate Laboratory at the University of Wisconsin, under the direction of Dr. Harry Harlow, some very interesting observations have been made about the behavior of monkeys and what it implies about children. Some of the baby monkeys were given terry-cloth-covered manikins as mother-substitutes. It seems that the comfort of the manikins met all the initial urgencies of feeling of the monkeys while they were growing up. But when they reached the age to find mates and become parents themselves, they failed. What was the reason for this neurotic behavior? Was it due to the fact that the manikins were not real mothers? Perhaps. Another possibility has been explored. The monkeys with the manikins were reared in separate cages where they could hear and see other monkeys but could not mix and play with them. It was discovered that

... regardless of mothering or lack of it, infants who have a chance to play with other little monkeys for periods as short as twenty minutes a day become socially normal monkeys. Even the offspring of the brutal mothers from the manikin experiment show no serious maladjustment ... On the other hand, all of the monkeys who were cut off from contact with playmates were unable to interact normally with other monkeys, socially or sexually.

Dr. Harlow states, "Our experiments suggest that the chance to play freely with other children is as important as mothering."[1]

First, then, reconciliation and the harmony that it produces must be experienced by the individual as a normal routine. This is what happens to monkeys and children who experience themselves through experiencing their playmates. Simple techniques and skills emerge which are regarded as the child's direct reaction to his immediate play environment. He learns how to belong and the fearful price of isolation. His general experience with the group becomes a part of his formal intent as a member of the group. Association with others, contacts with fellowship, this is the setting in which recognition of the need to be cared for emerges and may become a part of the working purpose of the individual in defining and determining the quality of his own relationships. He accepts

[1] *This Week Magazine*, "What Monkeys Are Teaching Science about Children," March 3, 1963, p. 18.

the fact that, whatever others' behavior toward him may seem to be, or however contradictory the problem, the real issue always is the same—the other person's need to be cared for must be honored. Behind all his hostility, hate, and antisocial behavior, the hunger persists—the ache to be cared for, for oneself alone.

> If I knew you and you knew me,
> And each of us could clearly see
> By the inner light divine,
> The meaning of your life and mine,
> I am sure that we would differ less
> And clasp our hands in friendliness—
> If I knew you and you knew me.[2]

Let us keep clearly in mind the issue here. The need to be cared for is fundamental to human life and to psychic and spiritual health and well-being. When this need is not met, the individual is thrown into conflict, an inner conflict that can only be resolved when the need is honored. The conflict expresses itself in many ways, from profound mental disturbance to the complete projection upon others of the hate and violence the person himself is feeling. The individual experiences the fulfillment of his need in a diffused way, by living in an atmosphere of acceptance and belonging. It is here that simple techniques of co-operation and adjustment are developed, which in time become the channels through which the intent to honor this deep need in others is implemented. Unwillingness to accept ill will, hatred, or violence directed toward oneself from another as the fundamental intent is the role of the reconciler, the function of reconciliation. "Father, forgive them, for they know not what they do," says Jesus as he is dying on the cross.

2.

One of the forms that reconciliation takes is what is generally known as nonviolence, that is, a response to a violent act, directed

---

[2] "At Church Next Sunday," author unknown, from *The Best Loved Religious Poems*, James Gilchrist Lawson, ed. (Westwood, N. J.: Fleming H. Revell Co., 1933).

toward oneself in the first place, in a manner that meets the need of the individual to be cared for, to be understood, rather than the apparent nature of the act itself. The term "violence" usually carries with it the connotation of physical force of some sort. Violence as physical force, when employed directly in face-to-face encounter, may be overwhelming and compelling. It is quick, decisive, and definite. There is a certain limited efficiency in its use. It tends to inspire fear and often makes for temporary capitulation. Its central purpose is to make it possible for one man to impose his will on another. As an instrument of national policy, its purpose is to impose one nation's will on another nation.

There is a very interesting and instructive discussion of violence in Ortega y Gasset's *The Revolt of the Masses,* where it is suggested that violence is always present, in fact or threat, in all human relations. The thing that distinguishes the barbarian from the civilized man is the priority given to the use of it. The civilized man postpones violence until all other methods are exhausted; while the barbarian resorts to it as soon as his will is thwarted.

It is well to remember that the violent act is the desperate act. It is the imperious demand of a person to force another to honor his desire and need to be cared for, to be understood. In this sense the violent act is a plea, a begging to have one's need to belong fulfilled and confirmed. For this reason, to confine the definition of violence to its physical expression is too restricting and limiting. Defenses against physical violence may be built and maintained until the individual is exhausted in death. Terrible as it is, it is not violence in its worst form. No. Violence at its worst may be nonphysical. Love itself may be a form of nonphysical violence. Many years ago I read an article in a magazine called *The World Tomorrow* describing an early experience of Mahatma Gandhi when he was the head of a school for boys. The sense of community between himself and the boys had been ruptured by a lie one of them told. Instead of punishing the boy directly, Gandhi announced that *he* would do penance for this by fasting for twenty-four hours. What was an act of nonviolence as far as the offender was concerned was an act of violence on Gandhi's body. Emotionally, it must have been a devastating experience for the hapless boy and the others.

The effect of nonviolence on the offender is apt to be so threatening that the security he feels in the violent act deserts him and he is thrown back upon the naked hunger of his own heart to be cared for, to be understood, to experience himself in harmony with his fellows. When violence is met with violence, the citadel of the spirit it not invaded. The most that is accomplished is a limited truce—a standoff—a stalemate. The fact of isolation becomes a way of life. All communication breaks down, and slowly the spirits of men become asphyxiated. For this reason, the only thing that can maintain the mood of violence between men beyond the heat and excitation of direct encounter is hatred. Hate is the great insulator, making it possible for one man to deny the existence of another or to *will* his nonexistence. Since the necessity to honor one's need to be cared for cannot be fundamentally denied, the only recourse left to the hater is to will the very nonexistence of the other person. Violence is the act through which such a will is implemented, and hate is its dynamic.

The very act of affirming the nonexistence of another human being is at once, in positive terms, an act of self-affirmation. Hate may become the basis of one's own self-estimate when one is faced with the will to one's own nonexistence. When a man is despised and hated by other men and all around are the instruments of violence working in behalf of such attitudes, then he may find himself resorting to hatred as a means of salvaging a sense of self, however fragmented. Under such circumstances, hate becomes a man's way of saying that he is present. Despite the will to his nonexistence on the part of his environment or persons in it, he affirms himself by affirming the nonexistence of those who so regard him. In the end the human spirit cannot tolerate this. Men are made for each other, and any sustained denial of this elemental fact of life cannot stand.

Thus nonviolence occurs and recurs on the horizon throughout man's life. It is one of the great vehicles of reconciliation because it creates and maintains a climate in which the need to be cared for and understood can be honored and effectively dealt with. The mood of nonviolence is that of reconciliation. It engenders in the individual an attitude that inspires wholeness and integration within. It provides the climate in which the things that are needed for peace, or for one's own peace, may be sensed, disclosed, and developed. It presupposes that the desire to be cared for and to care for others is one with the very essence of all one's meaning and significance. It thus provides a working atmosphere in which this mutual desiring may be normal, reasonable, and accepted.

But nonviolence is not merely a mood or climate, or even an attitude. It is a technique and, in and of itself, a discipline. In the first place, it is a rejection of physical force, a renunciation of the tools of physical violence. These may be renounced because they are not available; such a renunciation has only tactical significance. Here nonviolence may be used effectively by violent men as a practical necessity. In this sense it has the same moral basis as violence. This is one of the ancient weapons of the weak against the strong and is a part of the over-all tactic of deception. It is instructive to note that when noviolence is used in this way in response to external necessity, this may not at all vitiate its creative impact upon those against whom it is used. The importance of this cannot be overemphasized. Because nonviolence is an affirmation of the *existence* of the man of violent deeds, in contradistinction to the fact that violence embodies a will to *nonexistence*, the moral impact which nonviolence carries may potentially realize itself in a given situation by rendering the violent act ineffective and bringing about the profoundest kind of change in attitude. All this may take place in encounter, even though the users of nonviolence are full of violence themselves. This is apt to be true in situations where the tools for physical violence are not available, or because even if used, the chances for their success are poor. It is entirely possible for an individual to use nonviolence with detachment—as an effective weapon and a substitute for weapons of violence—while the mood continues to be violent, a mood that inspires hate, that wills the nonexistence of another. The logic of hate is to kill. It is to translate the willing of the nonexistence of another into the literal deed of his extermination. Men who war against each other, if they are to be effective in their undertaking, must hate. They must will the nonexistence of each other. Once this happens, all moral responsibility disappears and they are free to do *anything* to them, to perform any act of violence or outrage upon them, without undermining their own sense of worth or value. Nonviolence and nonkilling mean, therefore, essentially the same thing.

In the second place, nonviolence may be a rejection not merely of the *physical* tools of violence—since their use is aimed at the destruction of human life, which is the ultimate denial of the need to be cared for—but also of the *psychological* tools of violence as well. Here we assume that, even if the tools of physical violence were available and could be of tactical significance, their use would be renounced because their purpose is to kill—to make good the will for the nonexistence of another human being. And this is to cut off his chances for actualizing of his potential sometime in his living future by dealing with him in the present.

But the psychological tools of nonviolence are of another order. Their purpose is to open the door of the heart so that what another is feeling and experiencing can find its way within. They assume that it is possible for a man to get real insight into the meaning of his deeds, attitudes, or way of life as they affect the life of his fellows. A man faced with nonviolence is forced to deal with himself, finally; every way of escape is ultimately cut off. This is why there can be no possible limit as to time or duration of nonviolent acts. Their purpose is not merely to change an odious situation, but, further, to make it urgent for a man to face himself in his action. Finally all must face the same basic question: Is what I am doing an expression of my fundamental intent toward any man when I am most myself? The more persistent nonviolent acts become, the more threatening they are to the person who refuses to deal with the ultimate question.

What then are some of the nonphysical tools of nonviolence? One is the will to refrain from the automatic response to violence: to fight or to flee. I use the word "tool" here advisedly. It is a graphic reconditioning of an ancient behavior pattern on the basis of which the survival of the species has been possible. It is a deliberate training or disciplining of the nervous patterns of the organism to a new kind of response. It places upon them the demand to absorb violence rather than to counteract it in kind. In initiating this procedure or process a person may know naked fear for the first time in life. He is threatened below the threshold of all his inherited defenses, and for a timeless moment is completely vulnerable and exposed. There is rioting in the streets of the soul, and the price of tranquility comes terribly high. Order and reconciliation must be restored within—here the major conquest must be achieved. At such a moment one is not dealing with a perpetrator of violence, a violent man, but with the stark fact of violence itself. This has to be conquered first. Once that has happened the power of the violent man is broken.

This principle is illustrated in a firsthand experience told by an undergraduate student who participated in sit-in demonstrations in one of the southern cities. She was one of several students who made up a team assigned to a particular drugstore to cover the lunch counter. As soon as they entered the store the lunch counter was cleared of all white patrons and closed. After about half an hour had elapsed, she noticed that down at the lower end of the counter the rope had been removed and, rather surreptitiously, white patrons were being permitted to come through and sit for service. Immediately she left her position and went down to the other end where the service was beginning. Just as she started to take a seat, a man who had been standing quietly against the wall sprang forward and ordered her to remove herself. This he did in the name of the law. Quietly she asked him to identify himself, since he was in plain clothes. He opened his coat to reveal his badge of authority. Whereupon the young lady said, "That's not a ——— County badge; you have no jurisdiction here." Nonplused, the officer seized her by the wrist, his fingers biting into her flesh, and pushed her up against the wall, holding her there. What follows now are her words as nearly as I can recall.

"It was my very first direct encounter with real violence. All the possibilities of what we were up against had been drilled into us in our training and every conceivable kind of situation had been simulated; but even so, I was not prepared for the stark panic that moved through me. This passed quickly and in its place I felt an intense and angry violence—but something in me held. I looked him in the face until I felt his fear and sensed his own anguish. Then I thought, now quite calmly, how desperate a man must be to behave this way to a defenseless girl. And a strange peace came over me and I knew now that violence could be taken, and that I could take it and triumph over it. I suppose that as long as I live I will be winning and losing this battle with myself."

The spirit of retaliation must be relaxed and overcome. Here again the reconciliation must go on in a man's spirit before he can be at one with the technique of nonviolence he employs as an instrument for social change. The spirit of retaliation is rooted profoundly in the total history of the race. It has an instinctual ground. Some of the latest findings of cultural anthropologists make the point very clearly that man's immediate ancestors were not peaceful root- and fruit-eating primates but predatory, territory-seeking animals. The conflict between the positive and creative inclination toward community and the positive and destructive inclination toward conquest seems to be older than the conscious life of mankind. Both inclinations have to do with survival. There is a quality in the spirit of reconciliation that heals the inner breaches by confirming the need to be cared for, to be held, honored in one's own life and in the lives of others. And this is the work of reconciliation. It begins with a man's own spirit. When he is challenged by the violent act, all kinds of feelings clamor to be heard. They appear singly and in fateful combination: fear in its many masks—of loss of face, loss of self-respect, loss of life; cowardice in all its subtleties—the futility of being a hero, the waste of energy on a situation that can only defeat one's true aim, one's vocational fulfillment; hate with all its self-affirming vitality when all other avenues of support are denied. At such a time a man may twist, turn, juggle and shift his ground, until at last he is face to face with his own sense of ultimate worth. This he puts over against the implication and intent of the violent act. Then, out of some deeper region than the mind, there begins to flow up into his spirit that which gives fresh courage, new strength, and wholeness. I do not understand this. I do not know how the miracle takes place when it does—all that I know is that such triumph is possible to the spirit of man.

Even so one may be mistaken. That is to say, the margin of self-deception is ever in flux. We are not quite sure that things are, in truth, as they seem to be in fact. We are therefore threatened by each new situation because it may reveal the awful magnitude of our previous self-deception. Hence it is most necessary for a man to try to establish some other-than-self reference in support of what seems to be his true state of being. Even as he seeks to do this, he knows that the validity of his inner peace and sense of triumph over the violent act does not depend on anything outside himself. But he must seek to establish it.

This brings our discussion at once to the primary function of nonviolence as a tool in the hands of a man of good will—as over against its use by a man of violence, as we saw earlier. The existential question is: How may the nonviolent attitude invade a violent situation and tame the wildness out of it?

It is not my purpose to explore extensively the considerable and growing literature on this subject, but rather to isolate some of the elements at work that can turn violence into a more harmonious situation and common feeling. Violence feeds on fear as its magic source of energy—the fear it engenders in those against whom it is directed. As long as men react to it with fear, their lives can be controlled by those in whose hands the instruments of violence rest. It is important in the etiquette of violence that the fear be centered around one's physical life and well-being or that of one's loved ones. By every cunning contrivance and subtlety, emphasis must be placed upon *physical* existence as the supreme good. All the conditioning that has gone into man's survival on the planet is in favor of such an emphasis. Once this is established, the only thing remaining for violence is to threaten to kill. If the highest premium is placed upon life, the fear of its loss or injury enables violence to maintain itself in active control over the lives of others. If there is no fear at this point, then the power of violence is critically undermined.

When there is a face-to-face encounter between nonviolence as a tool in the hands of a nonviolent man and violence as a tool in the hands of a violent man, the human element makes reconciliation a real potential in the situation. Unless the actual status of a human being as such is denied, reconciliation between people always has a chance to be effective. But when this status is denied, a major reappraisal or reassessment must take place *before* the work of reconciliation—which is the logic of nonviolence—can become effective.

Is there anything about the nonviolent act itself that can do this? The moral impact of nonviolence on violent men cannot be denied. There is a strange alchemy and contagion about courage in the face of danger that threatens and imperils. It awakens, first, a kind of admiration which is often apt to develop into subtle identification. In one of Olive Schreiner's books telling of her early experiences as a girl in South Africa, she tells of her reaction to a story about a woman who led African men against a group of armed European soldiers. The soldiers had guns but the Africans had only spears and shields made of hide. But with her inspiration, they marched up the hill under the terrible aegis of her courage until the last man died. Another story had to do with a woman whose husband brought back to his hut a new wife, to the shame and dishonor of his present wife and little child. Next day, early in the morning, the mother took her child to a high hill overlooking a rocky ledge and there, with the child in her arms, jumped to their death. The author writes that the courage of these two women settled for her forever the fact that community between her and the black women transcended all barriers that separated black from white in her South Africa.

Again and again we find that courage does this in the face of violence—it awakens admiration and then identification. Once this has happened, the grounds of reconciliation are established. For meaningful situations of community must be established. Courage is only one of them. Experiences of meaning which people share are more compelling than the barriers that separate them. If such experiences can be multiplied over a time interval of sufficient duration, then any barrier between men, of whatever kind, can be undermined. Thus the way of reconciliation is opened.

The problem is of a slightly different order if the violence is impersonal. One cannot, merely by a personal attitude of nonviolence, effect reconciliation in a violent system. A way has to be found to personalize the system. The fact that a system is violent has to be brought home to those who are largely in control of the power structure of which it is a collective expression. This demands more than the discipline of the nonviolent person. The techniques of nonviolence must be employed. In recent years wide use of such techniques has been so much in evidence that a new group of words has come into the vocabulary—"sit-ins," "walk-ins," "pray-ins," etc., not to speak of the familiar "boycott." It is in connection with these that the individual is apt to meet violence directly—notwithstanding the fact that the technique is aimed at a violent system rather than at violent individuals.

The purpose of his use of nonviolence as a collective device is to awaken conscience and an awareness of the evil of a violent system, and to make available the experience of the collective destiny in which all people in the system are participating. There is always the possibility that the effect of the nonviolent technique will be to solidify and organize the methods of violence used in counteraction. There is nothing unnatural here. Clearly, if the system is altered along the lines of the needs of those who are practicing nonviolence, then a profound change has to take place within the power structure so that *all* may share the fruits of the common life. The resistance to nonviolence discussed here is the last line of defense of those who cannot yet understand or feel that the ancient need to be cared for and understood, and to care for and understand, is asserting itself. And this is, at last, the work of reconciliation. The discipline for all who are involved has the same aim—to find a way to honor what is deepest in one person and to have that person honor what is deepest in the other.

3.

The discipine of reconciliation for the religious man cannot be separated from the discipline of religious experience. In religious experience a man has a sense of being touched at his inmost center, at his very core, and this awareness sets in motion the process that makes for his integration, his wholeness. It is as if he saw into himself, beyond all his fragmentation, conflicts, and divisiveness, and recognized his true self. The experience of the prodigal son is underscored in the religious experience of the race—when he came to himself, he came to his father's house and dwelling place. The experience of God reconciles all the warring parts that are ultimately involved in the life of every man as against whatever keeps alive the conflict, and its work is healing and ever redemptive. Therefore there is laid upon the individual the need to keep the way open so that he and his Father may have free and easy access to each other.

Such is the ethical imperative of religious experience. This is not to suggest that religion is the only basis of the ethical imperative, but to state clearly that such an imperative is central to the religious experience. "So if you are offering your gift at the altar, and there remember that your brother has something against you, leave your gift there before the altar and go; first be reconciled to your brother, and then come and offer your gift" (Matt. 5:23-24).

What a man knows as his birthright in his experience before God he must accept and confirm as his necessity in his relations with his fellows. It is in the presence of God that he feels he is being *totally* dealt with, that the words of the Psalmist find a resting place in his own heart: Thou hast "not dealt with us according to our sins, nor rewarded us according to our iniquities" (Ps. 103:10). The sins, bitterness, weakness, virtues, loves, and strengths are all gathered and transmuted by His love and His grace, and we become whole in His Presence. This is the miracle of religious experience—the sense of being totally dealt with, completely understood, and utterly cared for. This is what a man seeks with his fellows. This is why the way of reconciliation and the way of love finally are one way.

At the beginning of our discussion reference was made to the fact that the building blocks for the society of man and for the well-being of the individual are the fundamental desire to understand others and to be understood. The crucial sentence is, "Every man wants to be cared for, to be sustained by the assurance of the watchful and thoughtful attention of others." Such is the meaning of love.

Sometimes the radiance of love is so soft and gentle that the individual sees himself with all harsh lines wiped away and all limitations blended with his strengths in so happy a combination that strength seems to be everywhere and weakness is nowhere to be found. This is a part of the magic, the spell of love. Sometimes its radiance kindles old fires that have long since grown cold from the neglect of despair, or new fires are kindled by a hope born full-blown without beginning and without end. Sometimes the same radiance blesses a life with a vision of its possibilities never before dreamed of or sought, stimulating new endeavor and summoning all latent powers to energize the life at its inmost core.

But there are other ways by which love works its perfect work. There is a steady anxiety that surrounds man's experience of love. It may stab the spirit by calling forth a bitter, scathing self-judgment. The heights to which it calls may seem so high that all incentive is lost and the individual is stricken with utter hopelessness and despair. It may throw in relief old and forgotten weaknesses to which one has made the adjustment of acceptance—but which now stir in their place to offer themselves as testimony of one's unworthiness and to challenge the love with their embarrassing reality. At such times one expects love to be dimmed, in the mistaken notion that it is ultimately based upon merit and worth.

Behold the miracle! Love has no awareness of merit or demerit; it has no scale by which its portion may be weighed or measured. It does not seek to balance giving and receiving. Love loves; this is its nature. This does not mean that it is blind, naïve, or pretentious, but rather that love holds its object securely in its grasp, calling all that it sees by its true name but surrounding all with a wisdom born both of its passion and its understanding. Here is no traffic in sentimentality, no catering either to weakness or to strength. Instead, there is robust vitality that quickens the roots of personality, creating an unfolding of the self that redefines, reshapes, and makes all things new. Such an experience is so fundamental that an individual knows that what is happening to him can outlast all things without itself being dissipated or lost.

Whence comes this power which seems to be the point of referral for all experience and the essence of all meaning? No created thing, no single unit of life, can be the source of such fullness and completeness. For in the experience itself a man is caught and held by something so much more than he can ever think or be that there is but one word by which its meaning can be encompassed—God. Hence the Psalmist says that as long as the love of God shines on us undimmed, not only may no darkness obscure, but we may find our way to a point in other hearts beyond all weakness and all strength, beyond all that is good or evil. There is nothing outside ourselves—no circumstance, no condition, no vicissitude—that can ultimately separate us from the love of God or of one another. And we pour out our gratitude to God that this is so!

The appearance of love may be used as a technique of social control or for the manipulation of other people while the manipulator himself has no sense of personal involvement. The ethic may become divorced from the spiritual and/or religious commitment out of which it comes, by which it is inspired. In other words, instead of being a moral imperative it can become a moral pretension. The love ethic may become a love dogma or doctrine, to which the mind may make an intellectual adjustment and to which mere mental assent may be given. This is one of the real perils when the ethic becomes incorporated in a system or in the organizational structure of an institution.

The reason for this is not far to seek. Neither a man nor an institution can embrace an ethical imperative without either becoming more and more expressive of it in the common life or developing a kind of increasing enmity to it. Here is the essential challenge of the modern world to the Christian Church.

What then is the nature of the discipline that love provides? In the first place, it is something that I must quite deliberately *want* to do. For many of us this is the first great roadblock. In our relations with each other there is often so much that alienates, that is distasteful; there seems to be every ground for refraining from the kind of concern that love demands. It is curious how we feel the other person must demonstrate a worthiness that commends itself to us before we are willing to *want* to move in outflow, in the self-giving that love demands. We want to be accepted just as we are, but at the same time we want the other person to *win* the right to our acceptance of him. This is an important part of the sin of pride. There must be genuine repentance for such an attitude. Forgiveness for this sin is the work of the grace of God in the human heart. A man seeks it before God and becomes aware of forgiveness only when, in his attitude toward his fellows, he comes to want to make available to them the consciousness of what God shares with him. God enables him to *want* to love. This is one of the reasons why I cannot separate the discipline of love from the discipline of religious experience.

In the second place, I must find the opening or openings through which my love can flow into the life of the other, and at the same time locate in myself openings through which his love can flow into me. Most often this involves an increased understanding of the other person. This is arrived at by a disciplined use of the imagination. We are accustomed to thinking of imagination as a useful tool in the hands of the artist as he reproduces in varied forms what he sees beyond the rim of fact that circles him round. There are times when it is regarded merely as a delightful, whimsical trait of the "childish mind." Our judgment trembles on the edge of condescension, pity, or even ridicule when imagination is confused with fancy in reports of the inner workings of the mind of the "simpleton" or "fool." But we recognize and applaud the bold, audacious leap of the mind of the scientist when it soars far out beyond what is known to fix a beachhead on distant, unexplored shores. But the imagination shows its greatest powers as the *angelos* of God in the miracle it creates when one man, standing on his own ground, is able while there to put himself in another man's place. To send his imagination forth to establish a point of focus in another man's spirit, and from that vantage point so to blend with the other's landscape that what he sees and feels is authentic—this is the great adventure in human relations. Yet this is not enough. The imagination must report its findings accurately, without regard for all previous prejudgments and private or collective fears. And even this is not enough. There must be both a spontaneous and a deliberate response to such knowledge which will result in the sharing of resources at their deepest level.

Very glibly we are apt to use such words as "sympathy," "compassion," "sitting where they sit," but in experience it is genuinely to be rocked to one's foundations. We resist making room for considerations that will bend us out of the path of preoccupation with ourselves, our needs, our problems. We corrupt our imagination when we give it range over only our own affairs. Here we experience the magnification of our own wills, the distortion of our own problems, and the enlargement of the areas of our misery. The activity of which we deprive our imagination in the work of understanding others turns in upon ourselves with disaster and sometimes terror.

The willingness to be to another human being what is needed at the time the need is most urgent and most acutely felt—this is to participate in a precise act of redemption. This is to stand for one intimate moment *in loco dei* in the life of another—that is, to make available to another what has already been given us. We are not the other person; we are ourselves. All that he is experiencing we can never know—but we can make accurate soundings which, properly read, will enable us to be to him what we could never be without such awareness. To the degree to which our imagination becomes the *angelos* of God, we ourselves may become His *instruments*. As the apostle says in the Phillips translation: "My prayer for you is that you may have still more love—a love that is full of knowledge and wise insight. I want you to be able always to recognize the highest and best, and to live sincere and blameless lives until the day of Jesus Christ" (Phil. 1:9-10).

In the third place, there must be a sense of leisure out of which we relate to others. The sense of it is far more important than the fact of leisure itself. Somehow it must be conveyed to the other person that our effort to respond to his need to be cared for is one with our concern to be cared for ourselves. Despite the pressures under which we live, it is entirely possible to develop a sense of leisure as the climate in which we function. We cannot be in a hurry in matters of the heart. The human spirit has to be explored gently and with unhurried tenderness. Very often this demands a reconditioning of our nervous responses to life, a profound alteration in the tempo of our behavior pattern. Whatever we learn of leisure in the discipline of silence, in meditation and prayer, bears rich, ripe fruit in preparing the way for love. Failure at this point can be one of unrelieved frustration. At first, for most of us, skill in tarrying with another has to be cultivated and worked at by dint of much self-discipline. At first it may seem mechanical, artificial, or studied, but this kind of clumsiness will not remain if we persist. How indescribably wonderful and healing it is to encounter another human being who listens not only to our words, but manages, somehow, to listen to *us*. Everyone needs this and everyone needs to give it, as well—thus we come full circle in love.

If all this is true, then it is clear that any structure of society, any arrangement under which human beings live, that does not provide maximum opportunities for free-flowing circulation among one another, works against social and individual health. Any attitudes, private or group, which prohibit people from coming into "across-the-board" contact with each other work against the implementation of the love ethic. So considered, segregation, prescriptions of separation, are a disease of the human spirit and the body politic. It does not matter how meaningful the tight circle of isolated security may be, in which individuals or groups move. The very existence of such circles, whether regarded as a necessity of religious faith, political ideology, or social purity, precludes the possibility of the experience of love as a part of the necessity of man's life.

The experience of love is either a necessity or a luxury. If it be a luxury, it is expendable; if it be a necessity, then to deny it is to perish. So simple is the reality, and so terrifying. Ultimately there is only one place of refuge on this planet for any man—that is in another man's heart. To love is to make of one's heart a swinging door.

CPSIA information can be obtained
at www.ICGtesting.com
Printed in the USA
BVHW082117030822
643755BV00001B/25